MAKING RCIA WORK

Geoffrey Chapman Pastoral Studies Series

Making RCIA work, handling the management of change and loss, parish evangelization, diocesan renewal, moral theology at the end of the twentieth century, the challenges raised by *Christifideles Laici*, reconciliation, these are all issues to be covered in the Geoffrey Chapman Pastoral Studies series.

For the clergy, pastoral workers and interested lay people, the series is based on experience, and provides a comprehensive introduction to the issues involved.

The authors are recognized authorities on their subjects and bring their considerable experience and expertise to bear on the series.

ALREADY PUBLISHED IN THE SERIES:

Grieving for Change:
A Spirituality for Refounding Gospel Communities
Gerald Arbuckle SM

Called to Mission
Christine Dodd

New Directions in Moral Theology
Kevin Kelly

MAKING RCIA WORK

*An Anthology of Material for
Use in RCIA Groups*

CHRISTINE DODD

GEOFFREY
CHAPMAN

Geoffrey Chapman

A Cassell imprint
Villiers House, 41/47 Strand, London, WC2N 5JE

First published 1993

British Library Cataloguing-in-Publication Data
A catalogue entry for this book is
available from the British Library.

ISBN 0–225–66662–6

Phototypeset by Intype, London
Printed and bound in Great Britain by Biddles Ltd, Guildford and King's
Lynn

CONTENTS

To
the people of the Diocese of Hallam,
in whose parishes this material came to life

ACKNOWLEDGEMENTS

I am grateful to the following authors and publishers for permission to reprint their material (with varying degrees of adaptation):

The Rite of Christian Initiation of Adults (Geoffrey Chapman).
Nigel Bavidge, *The Sacraments Explained* (Kevin Mayhew).
Anne Bishop and Eldon Hay, *Telling My Story, Sharing My Faith* (United Church of Canada).
Christine Dodd, *Called to Mission* (Geoffrey Chapman).
Christine Dodd, *Making Scripture Work* (Geoffrey Chapman).
Christine Dodd, *The Immortal Diamond* (Darton, Longman and Todd).
Deborah Jones, *Focus on Faith* (Kevin Mayhew).
Telling the Story, Sharing the Faith (Board of Mission and Unity of the General Synod of the Church of England).
Towards Deeper Faith (Catholic Adult Education Service, Archdiocese of Adelaide).
Sarum Primer.

All Scripture quotations are from the New Revised Standard Version of the Bible, copyright 1946, 1952, 1971 by the Division of Christian Education of the National Council of the Churches of Christ in the USA.

Every effort has been made to contact the owners of copyright material and we hope that no copyright has been infringed. Pardon is sought and apology made if the contrary be the case, and a correction will be made in any reprint of this book.

INTRODUCTION

A great deal of material is available about the Rite of Christian Initiation of Adults; nevertheless, this book proved to be extremely difficult to compile. One of the reasons for this was the very nature of RCIA itself. 'A process and not a programme' has been the rallying call of those of us who have been involved with parishes and groups over the years. To produce a book which possessed a structure and yet did not give the impression of being a programme was not easy. Even now my fear is that, despite my efforts to dissuade people from doing this, it will be used as such.

A second difficulty lay in the need to provide a structure for the sessions while ensuring that they could be easily adapted to meet specific needs. Most, though not all, of the sessions in the book follow a similar pattern, although not always in the same order. First, some way of introducing the theme ('About ourselves'). Second, some means of giving information ('Input'). Brief notes only are given for this. Third, some way of helping people relate the theme to their own lives. In addition, some suggestions for prayer are given, usually at the end of the session. (It is assumed that opening prayers will be said and no suggestions are made for these.) Every parish will have to decide how to adapt all this to its own situation. It has been a pattern which I have found works well *provided* it is not the *only* pattern and provided the leaders are sensitive enough to the group and to its needs. In particular, attention must be given to the language we use. Detailed theological language will be foreign to many people. We also need to be sensitive to the fact that some people may find writing or reading difficult or unhelpful. In the same way care needs to be taken over the group work part of a session. Not everyone is happy in a small group. Working in pairs, threes or fours sometimes helps, as does leaving the group as one unit. Variety is needed in this as in most forms of good Christian adult education.

Anyone picking up this book will soon see that it does not cover everything. It is not a compendium of sessions that deal with the whole of Christian doctrine! Some areas are not covered at all. Others are covered more than once in several different ways. The fact that no session is provided on a specific topic is not a sign that I did not think it important. A parish RCIA process should not be made into a sort of 'hold-all' designed to carry everything all at once. Each parish must make up its own mind what needs to be omitted and what needs to be added.

Finally, two words of thanks need to be said. First, to Anne King at Geoffrey Chapman for her continual support and gentle encouragement when my enthusiasm waned and for many helpful comments on the text. Second, to those groups who have worked with the material. It has to be said that this book has been compiled rather than written. It comprises tried and tested material which has been gathered together from groups and parishes of many different kinds. Without them this book would not have been possible. To these groups, especially those within the Diocese of Hallam where most of the material was used, I would like to express my thanks and appreciation. They have ensured that the material in this book really does 'make RCIA work'.

Christine Dodd

Chapter 1

TRAVELLING WITH RCIA

When a book begins with a general outline or introduction to a subject there is a great temptation for the reader to ignore it and skip to the 'real issues'. If that temptation is present, please resist it, for this book is about only *part* of the RCIA process and the chapters that follow must be put into the context of the whole of the RCIA journey.

This book is not a complete guide to RCIA and certainly should not be used as a 'programme'. It is specifically designed to cover one element in the RCIA process – the work done in groups and the interaction that takes place within them. RCIA is, of course, much wider than this, though in my experience too many parishes put so much emphasis on the group side of the process that it effectively becomes all there is. Indeed, too many parishes do not see RCIA as a process at all but as a programme to be got through, often according to a book. As a consequence it becomes very like the old-style convert instruction, only it happens to take place within a small group instead of on a one-to-one basis. This style of working is not RCIA.

It is because there is so much more to the RCIA process than what happens in the group meetings that we need to see the overall picture. This is bound to be the 'bare bones', a sort of skeleton around which we put the flesh of the process, but such an overview should help put the work we do in groups into perspective.

RCIA, the process – basic principles

The Rite of Christian Initiation of Adults is commonly described as the Adult Catechumenate celebrated in stages. This sounds very formal and off-putting. In fact, it is the way of welcoming, forming and initiating new members into the Church.

My experience in working with many parishes using the RCIA is that there are three cardinal principles which run through everything. All three are about 'wholeness'. First, RCIA is not an extra programme that a parish may decide to run as part of its adult education work. RCIA seeks to involve the whole community: it is a whole-parish affair. This is far removed from the concept of the would-be 'convert' having private sessions with the parish priest and then being left to sink or swim in a congregation of people he or she may not have properly met, let alone know. In this process we celebrate together as the journey for the whole parish continues. We learn from each other as we share stories of faith and what the teaching of the Church means for us as a group, as well as for individuals.

A second principle is that RCIA is about another kind of 'wholeness'. It is about recognizing that there is more to faith than presenting people with a sort of intellectual assault course to be got through in order to take part in the full life of the Church. Rather, RCIA presents us with the theory and practice that faith is living and growing within each one of us and each one of us is on a journey which goes on throughout life. The RCIA process introduces inquirers to a journey of faith on which we all are travellers. It is a journey on which we learn from one another. One of the joys of being part of the process is to see people, many of whom have been Catholics for years, coming to a new realization of what it means to have faith. It is therefore a blend of coming to new intellectual understanding *and* of discovering the difference this makes to the way we live our lives.

A third RCIA principle is that it recognizes that we come to a deeper knowledge of God in many different ways. We are people made up of emotion and objective thought, joy and pain, action and reflection. RCIA, therefore, stresses the importance of allowing people to have experiences of community, liturgy, discussion, listening, doing and being, to enable them to discover that faith is a way of life. It is to be lived in the company of others and involves the whole of our personalities. It seeks to give people knowledge about what the Church teaches *and* an awareness of what that means in terms of a living relationship with God.

These three principles, which I have described as having something to do with 'wholeness', can be seen in the basic structure to which we now turn. I shall outline each of the four stages. Each one has a technical name which may be difficult for those not already familiar with the process but do not be put off, it is not as complicated as it appears! At each stage,

(a) we look at the theory;
(b) to help us put the theory into a practical context we follow the story of one person, Paul, who made the RCIA journey;
(c) finally, we look at the practical questions of who does what, when, where and how, along with some questions for reflection.

The RCIA faith-journey – the four stages

Stage one – the pre-catechumenate and evangelization stage

The first stage of the RCIA journey concerns evangelization. It is assumed that the parish is, or should be, aware of its evangelizing role within the wider community. Evangelization is not something we can opt into or out of depending on our view. Rather, as the 1987 Synod of Bishops said:

> The task of evangelising all peoples constitutes the essential mission of the Church.

This task of evangelization belongs to all the baptized and not just to a few. It belongs to the community and so it is the community which should be the primary evangelizing tool. Hence the need for RCIA to be a whole-parish process.

Paul came into contact with St Mary's through his friend Gary. Gary and Paul had worked together in the same office until Gary moved to a new job. Paul would often visit him and, as Gary was a committed Catholic, it happened that one Sunday evening Paul went along with him to the usual Sunday Mass. Gary was somewhat anxious. Although St Mary's was a fairly active parish there was nothing very unusual about it. If he was honest he feared Paul would end up ridiculing him for his church-going. In fact he was right to have his doubts. Paul was completely at sea. It was all foreign to him. The words, the actions, the music, everything was unlike anything he had experienced before. But he was intrigued rather than dismissive. He knew Gary too well to believe that he would be involved in something that was a load of mumbo-jumbo, for his friend was a level-headed guy who enjoyed a good joke as much as the next man. When they got back to Gary's flat the questions started. Why did this happen? What was that for? What did the priest mean when he said that? and so on. Gary did his best to answer his friend's questions. Next time Paul came he invited some other members of the congregation around. This time the questions were more profound. Paul's younger sister had died the year before. Why, if there was a God of love, did he allow it? What about all the suffering in the world? Hadn't science and psychology proved that people no longer needed to believe in God at all?

As Paul continued to be interested, Gary suggested they should go together to the new meetings which were starting at St Mary's where they could share their discussions with a wider group and where they could hear what the Church had to say about it all. Paul was a bit reluctant but by now he knew several people connected with St Mary's and he was willing to give it a go. So it was that he started on the RCIA journey.

Paul, of course, had been on his journey of faith long before he found the Christian community. God had been at work a long time in him. This is an important point to remember for, whether we are long-standing Christians or new searchers, we all have a past during which God has been present. People do not start the RCIA process like empty bottles waiting to be filled. They come at different stages of understanding and with different experiences of faith. This first part of the process gives all those taking part the opportunity to hear the gospel afresh, or for the first time, and to discover where the journey is leading.

This period of the pre-catechumenate is therefore a time for:

discovering the inquirers' backgrounds;
discovering their questions and working with these;
the proclamation of the gospel.

This is truly the time for inquiry, for welcoming, for sharing stories of faith (our own and the Church's). It is a time to help people hear, perhaps for the first time, the message of the Good News of the saving love of Christ and to join with them in the journey of discovering what that means in their own lives.

WHO, WHEN, WHERE AND HOW?

Who?

The RCIA process depends greatly on the concept of 'shared ministry'. It recognizes that many, many people should be involved. Welcomers, catechists, musicians, sponsors, group leaders and many others as well as the priest are all directly involved. Others support with their prayers and their hospitality. The whole parish is part of the process. (One of the best methods of discovering the variety of gifts needed and available in the parish is to use *The Way We Were*; see the Bibliography on p. 130.) It is important that those directly involved discover a real sense of community in this early stage. Members of the congregation can often help by inviting candidates to their homes and making friends with them on a social level. At this stage of the process the candidates are called *Inquirers*.

When?

The length of time this first stage of the process takes is not specific. According to the needs of the inquirers it may take a few weeks or several months. Some people take several years. Most parishes use the autumn period for this stage but this will vary.

Where?

Again, circumstances will often dictate where this process takes place. It is important to remember that adults are most responsive when their surroundings are comfortable and pleasant. The good news of the gospel ill accords with dingy halls, unpleasant smells and cold draughts.

How?

This period of the proclamation of the good news is a time for discovering the background of the inquirers, discovering what God is doing in their lives and starting to answer their questions. Whatever is done must present the gospel as something living. It should help the inquirers to see where God fits in to their own life-journey and how they can respond to his call. It is important at this stage to answer any questions which people may have. This should be done promptly. Do not put people off because the subject will be dealt with in later sessions. We may not be able to reply fully but to answer by saying that 'We shall come to that in session 16' is no answer!

Also important in this stage (and throughout the process) is the use of some form of joint prayer and para-liturgy. No formal rites are specified for this time but there should be a chance for prayer suited to the needs of the inquirers.

In order to help us think through what this stage means for our own local church here are some questions which may help.

Questions for reflection

1. How welcoming is your parish?
2. How much time is spent keeping the parish ticking over and how much in reaching out to others?
3. In what ways is the word 'evangelization' translated into action in your parish?
4. Who are the people who should be involved in the RCIA process in your parish?

MOVING ON

At the end of this period a decision is called for on the part of both the inquirer and the Church. The inquirer must determine whether to continue the journey and to take the next steps on the road to following Christ within the Catholic Christian tradition. The Church must determine the inquirer's readiness and intention. If it is clear that God is calling the inquirer to the next stage of the journey, the Rite of Becoming a Catechumen is celebrated at this point.

This book is not concerned with the Rites themselves but one important point needs to be remembered here. The Rite of Becoming a Catechumen is for those who have *not* been baptized. In our situation it is common for people involved in the RCIA process to have already been baptized as infants in another Christian tradition but not to have practised their faith. These people cannot become catechumens, which is, after all, a pre-baptismal stage. They are often called candidates to distinguish them from catechumens.

The Catechumenate played an important part in the life of the early Church. People became catechumens before baptism, so that they were part of the Church but not yet baptized.

Today this part of the Church's life has been restored and forms the next part of RCIA.

Stage two – the Catechumenate

When the inquirers become catechumens they enter into a different relationship with the Church. This is made clear in the *Rite of Christian Initiation of Adults* (1987, p. 18):

> From this time on the Church embraces the catechumens as its own with a mother's love and concern. Joined to the Church, the catechumens are now part of the household of Christ, . . .

This second stage is a time for complete and elementary catechesis which leads to deeper faith. For Paul, the second stage of the journey began with his becoming a catechumen. He had never been baptized but many others undertaking the journey with him had been. By now he was familiar with the group which met each week in the parish centre, and they knew each other quite well. He found that there was a great deal more to Christianity than he had previously imagined. For Paul this period was one of consolidation and formation. He learnt a great deal about the way God speaks to his people through the Scriptures and the Church. He discovered more about the Church community of which he was now a part and he began to be involved in active work within the parish. He had a great gift for listening and he had discovered that not far from where he lived was a residential home for the elderly, which he now visited regularly along with another member of the congregation who had been doing so for several years.

WHO, WHEN, WHERE AND HOW?

Who?
In this stage the catechists, priests and teachers play an important part but, as is the case throughout the whole of the process, the community itself is vital. The role of *sponsors* is important too for they take the responsibility of accompanying the catechumen or candidate more closely.

When?
The Catechumenate, like the period of evangelization, can last for several weeks, months or years, depending on the needs

of the candidate. The candidates in this stage are called catechumens (although, as already mentioned, for those who have
already been baptized 'candidate' is often used).

Where?
The Catechumenate sessions are usually held in the same place
as the evangelization stage, but this need not necessarily be
so. In theory, and following the ancient tradition of the Church,
catechumens should not be present at the Eucharist after the
Liturgy of the Word. Some parishes do provide a separate
session for catechumens at this time, others do not. Some
catechumens prefer to make use of the opportunity of a separate session and should be given the choice to do so. The
Catechumenate is also marked by a series of rites designed to
implant in the lives of individuals the teaching they are receiving. This enables them to understand at first hand the worship
of the whole community and to discover the various actions,
signs and symbols which are manifestations of that worship.

How?
This period is one in which a great deal of discussion and
learning takes place. Sessions should be geared to ensuring
that the catechumens and candidates receive information in the
faith and an understanding of how God is working in their
lives and the life of the Church.

Questions for reflection
1. What do we want the catechumens and candidates to discover in this period?
2. How shall we go about achieving this?
3. Do we have parishioners blessed with the gift of teaching?

MOVING ON

At the end of the Catechumenate, the catechumen and the
Church must discern the readiness of the individual for the
sacraments of initiation. If it is clear that God is calling
the catechumen onward at this stage, the entry into the next
stage is celebrated at the Rite of Election. This takes place on
the First Sunday of Lent. In this celebration the names of the

catechumens are enrolled in the Book of the Elect. Often this Rite is carried out at a diocesan level by the bishop in the cathedral.

The candidates, now the Elect, enter the third stage.

Stage three – the Purification and Enlightenment stage

The third stage of the journey is a time for deeper conversion. It is a time for prayer, fasting and repentance and also for spiritual recollection. This period seems to have more to do with spirituality than with catechesis as such, but we must be careful not to make hard and fast distinctions here for too often we create a false dichotomy between the two.

This stage is one of intense spiritual preparation for the Easter sacraments, not just for the Elect but for the whole parish. It provides an opportunity to examine our lives in the light of the gospel and to hear the call to repentance and new beginnings.

For Paul this period began on the First Sunday of Lent when he became one of the Elect. The period of Purification and Enlightenment which followed was, for him, one of the most moving stages of the RCIA journey. He learnt much about what it meant to pray. He learnt too about the Lenten sacramentary and lectionary. He reflected on the great conversion stories in the gospels and discovered their relevance for his own life. He discovered the cost of following Christ and the way he could respond to his call in his own situation.

WHO, WHEN, WHERE AND HOW?

Who?

In this stage the godparents play an important part. Godparents are not necessarily the same people as sponsors. They testify for the Elect and continue to journey with them through the various stages of this part of the journey and on to the Rites of Initiation and beyond. Catechists and those with the particular gift of prayer are important too.

When?

Unlike the other stages of the journey which have no specific time scale, the period of Purification and Enlightenment takes place during Lent. It is therefore an intense period of personal and parish renewal.

Where?
As with the other stages this will vary according to circumstance but it is important that this period, which concentrates so much on spirituality and renewal, should take place in an atmosphere conducive to this.

How?
Many parishes change tack during this period and offer a different way of presenting this part of the Church's life. Flexibility is vital. Be prepared to experiment and remember that not everyone prays the same way or hears the call to repentance in one set pattern.

Questions for reflection
1. How can Lent be made a time of real personal and community renewal?
2. What do we want the Elect to discover during Lent?
3. What shall we do?
4. Who is going to be involved?

MOVING ON
During Lent the Rites provide for a number of *Scrutinies*. These are Rites designed to help the community and individuals scrutinize their lives in the light of the gospel. On the third Sunday of Lent the Elect are presented with a copy of the Creed, symbolizing the faith of the Church they are to profess. On the fifth Sunday of Lent they are given a copy of the Lord's Prayer, representing the prayer life of the Church. As the great three days of the Easter Triduum approach, the Sacrament of Reconciliation for those already baptized is celebrated. (This, of course, is not necessary for the unbaptized.) All these Rites, and the journey so far, culminate in the Sacraments of Initiation at the Easter Vigil when the Elect and candidates are baptized or received into full communion with the Church, as they are confirmed and partake fully in the Eucharist for the first time.

Stage four – post-baptismal catechesis or mystagōgia

The RCIA journey does not cease with the great initiation ceremonies. They are the start rather than the end. In the past it was common for new Christians (or neophytes) to be left to their own devices once they had become full members of the Church. RCIA avoids this by providing the opportunity of a period of post-baptismal catechesis. Called the mystagōgia or 'deepening of the mysteries' it enables new Christians to settle in to church life.

For Paul this period was important. He had made many new friends during the previous months and he still had many questions to ask. He also needed to find his feet as a practising member of the Church and to discover how he could use his own gifts and abilities within the community of the parish. This period provided him with a time when he could settle down and integrate into the community. The community saw in him much that would enrich its life. He had already done a great deal of visiting in a residential home for the elderly as a catechumen. Now he was taking someone else with him. The evangelized was becoming the evangelizer. Perhaps without realizing it Paul was bringing new life into his Church community and was to be the instrument of others coming to know something of the faith that he had discovered. During this time also Paul began to see something of the wider Church. One Thursday evening, just before Pentecost, the Bishop invited all those who had recently been baptized or received into the Church to come and meet him informally. It was a happy occasion which enabled Paul to obtain a wider view of the Church.

WHO, WHEN, WHERE AND HOW?

Who?

It is the community of the church itself which has the most important role to play in this stage. If that community is not welcoming and open, then integration into it will be difficult, if not impossible. The community also needs to recognize that the neophytes bring a vitality and freshness with them and that they should be allowed to assume their rightful place within the parish. Responsibilities and roles within the parish must be shared.

When?
This period usually lasts throughout Eastertide. Some parishes extend it for longer.

Where?
Although all group sessions may be held in one place during this period it may also be possible to move around within the parish. As the new members become involved and integrated they need to know how they can use their gifts and talents. Consequently, they need to see what happens within the various groups in the community and to discover how they, in their turn, can bring to the local church their own particular skills. It is the new richness brought by people like Paul which enables the church to be enlivened.

How?
This stage of the RCIA process, with its emphasis on integration into the community and the enlivening of it, requires some flexibility depending on the nature of the parish and the neophytes themselves. There should be some consideration of the Eastertide gospels and what it means to live out the Eucharist. Giving confidence to the neophytes is also important if they, in their turn, are to to become evangelizers.

Questions for reflection

1. How is the Christian community going to help the neophytes take their rightful place within it?

2. How will the community encourage the neophytes to enliven it?

3. How will the community help the neophytes discover their gifts and use them?

MOVING ON

The RCIA process is not linear, it is more like a spiral. A parish that takes RCIA seriously never does the same thing in exactly the same way again because at the end of the cycle the parish is never the same. It has new members, bringing new gifts and, in their turn, new people. So, RCIA is not a programme which can be repeated year after year without change. The next time Paul's parish undertakes the process it will be a different experience. The aims and objectives may remain the same but the way those are put into practice will certainly be different as the parish meets new people. This fluidity means that when planning for RCIA we can, and should, have clear guidelines but must always be prepared to change tack if necessary. People are more important than structures.

Guidelines

Given the way the process works, what guidelines can we discern? I suggest three general ones here and then two which are specific to the group work involved in the process, the real subject of this book.

1. COMMUNITY AWARENESS

One of the most important elements to consider when beginning RCIA is that of parish involvement and understanding. It is vital that the local Christian community comprehends the basis of the process and what it seeks to achieve. This is especially true because the whole ethos behind RCIA is that it is a whole-parish process and because the Rites should be celebrated at the main Liturgies when the whole community is gathered together. If the people of the parish do not have a clue about what is happening or why, then the scene is set for much grumbling and misunderstanding. Ways also need to be found to ensure good communication throughout the process so that the RCIA group does not become an 'in-group' doing its own thing. Possible ways forward might include:

(a) Use of sermons and bulletins.
(b) Talking to established parish groups (i.e. Union of Catholic Mothers, SVP, Social Activities group, etc.).
(c) Holding special parish meetings, either whole-parish meetings or house-group style.
(d) Establishing an RCIA photographic board (where the progress of the process can be recorded in picture form for all to see).
(e) Producing booklets or videos which explain what, why and how.

(f)   Providing opportunities for those who have experienced the process to talk about it to the whole congregation.

(g)   Using drama (see bibliography).

2. PLANNING

The next important element is planning. It is obvious that RCIA cannot be done by one person. It requires a whole team of people with different skills and abilities. The parish will have to decide:

(a)   Who will be involved? (This includes welcomers, teamakers, sponsors, catechists, etc.) How many people will you need?

(b)   Who will co-ordinate it all and how?

(c)   Where will it happen?

(d)   When will it start? How frequent will the meetings be and at what time?

(e)   What will be done and how?

(f)   How will the Rites be celebrated?

Such questions and many others will need to be addressed and adequate plans made.

3. FLEXIBILITY

The art of an effective RCIA process in the parish is the ability to adapt and adapt and adapt. If something which has been planned is simply not working then it is pointless to continue with it. People must come before our plans and their needs must be met. This does not mean that we lurch from crisis to crisis or allow a haphazard approach to rule. It means being open and watchful for any changes which may be necessary as the process unfolds.

Guidelines for groups

When it comes to work within the group sessions, two important factors must be remembered.

1. CONDITIONS

It is a well-known fact that adults learn best when their physical and psychological needs are met. In practice this means that people respond better if they are in surroundings where they feel comfortable, safe and welcome. Much could be written about this whole area. Suffice it to say that attention must be given to:

(a) The comfort of the facilities. Are we expecting people to sit on hard chairs in draughty rooms with dingy lighting? We are proclaiming a gospel of light, freedom, accessibility and joy. What message are we giving if we do not make people feel physically and mentally at home? What can we do to improve matters?

(b) The welcome given to people. A good deal of the RCIA work is done by sharing experiences and stories. Will people feel at home enough to do this? Who will help them? How?

(c) The space given to people. How will we handle situations where people need personal space to reflect? How will we deal with any conflict that arises because some want to go quicker than others?

2. SHAPE

The second guideline concerns the shape of each session. It is important that we do not do the same thing every time and work in the same way. People do not all learn in the same way or at the same pace. Some like to talk in groups, some loathe it. Some learn more by seeing than listening, some more by doing than by being passive. How do we take all this on board? How do we build in variety without it becoming so loose that it all falls apart?

I suggest that three elements are necessary in every session, no matter what methodology we use or what emphasis we place on particular styles. First there must be *a link with life*. RCIA is not about filling people up with learning and knowledge. It is about helping them to develop a real and living faith with God, of which learning facts is a part. That means that what they learn must be related to the life they live. Second there must be *input*. Sharing our own experiences is important but there must also be some input to help people onwards. Otherwise we can end up sharing our own ignorance with each other! This does not mean that each time there has to be a lecture. It does mean that there should be some way of giving new insights and sharing them within the group. We need a balance. People do need to be informed of the Church's teaching. They also need to see how that teaching is lived out. On the one hand, if we go overboard on the life experience, people will rightly complain that they are not getting enough 'meat'. On the other hand, if we provide no means of allowing people to make the teaching their own, they may well not see the relevance of it. Thirdly, there should be some *spirituality*. At the start this may be little more than an opening prayer but as time goes on the group should be encouraged not only to experience praying together in various ways but also to create such para-liturgies themselves.

The rest of this book consists of various outlines for use in groups which may or may not be valuable. There will almost certainly be a need to adapt them to individual circumstances, so they should not be lifted and used without careful consideration.

If I could liken what follows to anything it would be to a supermarket. No one doing the weekly shopping picks up every item from the supermarket shelves. Nor do people necessarily start putting items into the trolley from the very first shelf they see inside the door. If they are organized at all they know what they want, they search it out and they leave behind what is not for them. Once the item has been selected and taken home, many different ways will be found to make use of it. So with this book. Work out what you need, discard what you do not require and select what you do. If there *is* a session which you think will be of use, take it and adapt and adapt it until it becomes *your* session and not mine. Only if this is done will the material here really become a tool which is of benefit for you and, above all, for your group. Finally, what follows does not pretend to cover everything. There are bound to be subjects which you feel are important but which are not found here. Whatever you do, remember that RCIA is a process not a programme.

Chapter 2

TRAVELLING THE PILGRIM WAY

It will soon be clear to anyone using this book that it is not possible to use this chapter to cover the first stage of the RCIA process, the second for the next stage and so on. Apart from the fact that there is far too much material, some of it overlapping in content and methodology, it is deliberately grouped together in themes to ensure that the book cannot be used as a programme and to encourage parishes to develop their own structure, using this book as an aid.

This chapter presents a number of sessions on the theme of journey. They are not consecutive. The idea, as is the case with all the material in this book, is that of 'pick and choose' depending on the needs and on the structure the parish has planned for itself. It is hardly necessary to reiterate that people come before structures and flexibility is vitally important.

In this chapter there are a number of suggestions on the topics of:

Where am I going in life?
Who am I anyway?
How can I be free?
What is happiness?
What can I make of suffering?
How is it possible to believe in God and science?
What can we make of a mystery?
How does God call me?

Given the nature of these sessions they are obviously suited to the beginning of the process, but not necessarily so.

1. Where am I going?

AIM

To enable participants to picture where they have come from in their lives and where their priorities suggest they are going.

ABOUT OURSELVES

Use the 'milestone' drawing as the basis for a handout. Encourage people to look back on their own lives and record the important moments within them. Stress that they are doing this for their own personal reflection and they do not have to show it to anyone else unless they wish to do so.

Ask people to look at their charts once they have completed them and answer for themselves the questions:

What are the most important factors which have made you as you are?
Which ones were outside your control?
If you had the chance to do things differently, what would you do and why?

Encourage people to share their answers in pairs if they so wish.

INPUT

This should contain:

(a) an understanding that life is a journey – physical, mental and spiritual – and that we share this journey with others;
(b) an understanding that faith is a journey which grows and develops as we share it with others;
(c) a sharing of one team member's own journey.

GROUP WORK

In small groups ask people to discuss:
What sort of life do I want for the future? List three things.
or
In the future I would like to be ....

PRAYER TIME

Allow some silence for people to reflect on what they have learnt.

Use some form of prayer in which people can offer themselves to God afresh.

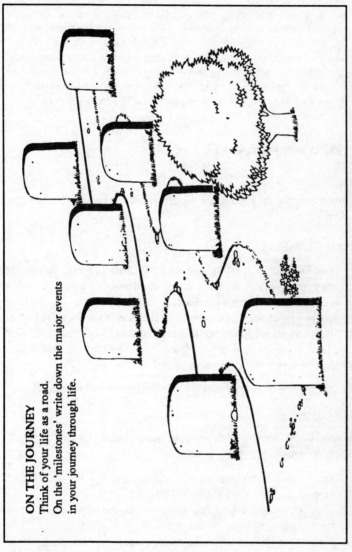

ON THE JOURNEY

Think of your life as a road.
On the 'milestones' write down the major events
in your journey through life.

From *Making Scripture Work* © 1989 Christine Dodd, published by Geoffrey Chapman (an imprint of Cassell Publishers Ltd) and Liturgical Press.

Notes

1. Notice the use of work in pairs. It is very important not to expect people to open up their innermost selves in large groups or even on a one-to-one basis with total strangers. Great sensitivity is needed here to ensure that people feel comfortable. No one should be forced to say anything if they do not wish to do so.
2. Notice the stress on journey. It is important to impress on people the idea that faith is living and growing and not a static possession.
3. Notice the personal story in the *Input*. People need to hear 'living stories' of how others have experienced the faith journey.

2. Who am I anyway?

AIM

To help people to recognize themselves as valued in the eyes of God.

ABOUT OURSELVES

(a) Ask people to turn to one another and say one thing that they are good at and one thing they are not good at. Allow a couple of minutes for this.
(b) In groups of four ask people to discuss how they feel when they are asked to do something they are good at, and why. How do they feel when they are asked to do something they are not good at, and why?

Summarize these responses on a flip-chart or blackboard.

INPUT

Use the story of the rich young man (Mark 10:17–22). From this story draw out these points:

(a) The young man was very good at keeping the commandments and for this Jesus loved him.
(b) The young man had his failures but he was not rejected for them.
(c) Jesus accepted the young man where he was on his faith journey. He knew that he could not make a response to what was asked of him at that time but he was not condemned. (Jesus' words about the rich are addressed to the crowd – not to the young man.)

GROUP WORK

1. Share together in pairs or small groups what good things in you Jesus looks at and loves.
2. What negative things in you does Jesus look at and love?
3. Allow that love to be part of you in the prayer time.

PRAYER TIME

Use the story in an imaginative way. Ask people to think of themselves as the rich young man. Encourage them to picture the scene and to enter into what was happening.

Notes

1. Notice the use of Scripture throughout the session. It is used for *both* exploration in the meeting and reflection in the prayer. It helps people see that Scripture can be used outside liturgy and has a living force for their lives.
2. Notice the use of pairs or very small groups. Many people find sharing difficult even in small groups. Group leaders may need to tell their own positive and negative elements to get people going and to give confidence. Again, those who wish to remain silent must be allowed to do so.

3. How can I be free?

AIM

To explore with the group the freedom Christ brings and what it means for our lives.

ABOUT OURSELVES

In pairs share one incident in your life where you felt out of control. This may be a major event or something quite small, as long as the experience of lack of control was clearly felt. In the wider group share some of the experiences associated with being out of control (e.g. fear, helplessness, anxiety, etc.).

INPUT

Use the story of the woman who was a sinner, from Luke 9:36–50. This woman was enslaved to her situation and unable to release herself from it.

Use the story to show:

(a)   the way she was enslaved, namely,
       by her circumstances
       by others' judgement of her
       by a lack of escape
       by her own sense of guilt

(b)   the way she was freed, namely,
       by Jesus' acceptance of her
       by his 'taking her side'
       by his offering her forgiveness

(c)   the way she found freedom, namely,
       by *believing* in Jesus' ability to help her
       by *trusting* Jesus to act on her behalf
       by *accepting* that the freedom he offered meant a new
       beginning

GROUP WORK

What do we want to be freed from? In practice, if we are to
find the freedom Jesus promised,

   what do we need to *believe* about Jesus?
   how do we need to *trust* in Jesus?
   what do we need to *accept* from Jesus?

PRAYER TIME

Place a lighted candle in a central position on a table. Give
everyone a small candle (unlit).

Allow people some time to reflect on any area of their own
life where they feel enslaved.

Encourage people to light their candle from the large one
and place it on the table as a sign of their trust in the God
who frees.

Close by saying a suitable prayer or singing a suitable hymn.

Notes

1.   Make sure you do not give the impression that freedom means
     'do as you like'. There is a responsibility involved in accepting
     the freedom Christ offers.
2.   Be sensitive to people who may feel very enslaved by some par-
     ticular event in their history or characteristic of their personalities.

Do not make people feel guilty if they do not feel 'free' at the end of the session. Freedom does not necessarily come all at once.

4. What is happiness?

AIM

The aim of this session is to help people explore what motivates them in their search for happiness.

ABOUT OURSELVES

Give people a blank piece of paper and ask them on their own to write or draw their answer to the question, 'If you could have anything in life, what would it be and why?' (If people are a little hesitant stress that there is no 'right' answer.)

In groups of four, give each group a pack of small cards on which are symbols and/or words to represent the following:

harmony with other people	seeing the best in all
love of family	faith
support of friends	sense of humour
money	health
knowledge of self	housing
support of church community	following conscience
knowledge of God	love for others

One or two blank cards should also be included.

Ask each group to arrange the cards in a pattern which best expresses for them what happiness means. They may use the blank cards to add their own symbols or words. (If you wish you can also provide them with a large sheet of paper to which the cards can be attached so that connecting lines, etc. can be added.)

Allow time for these discoveries to be shared in the whole group.

INPUT

This might include the following:

(a) True happiness comes from
    knowing we are loved
    loving in return
    accepting ourselves

(b) We search for harmony or wholeness.

(c) Christians believe that true happiness lies in a relationship with the God who made us.

God loves us to the uttermost.

He wishes us to love him in return.

Because God does this we can accept ourselves and discover the harmony or wholeness he wishes us to have.

GROUP WORK

Discuss:

(a) What causes us to be dis-eased (i.e., not at ease with ourselves)?

(b) What does our faith tell us about how God heals us?

PRAYER TIME

One member reads aloud Luke 18:35–43.

Invite people to hear Jesus saying to them 'What do you want me to do for you?' and to respond by making their own prayer in silence.

Quiet music could be played if people are unhappy with too much silence.

Close by sharing together the harmony God offers in the words of the Grace.

The grace of our Lord Jesus Christ and the love of God and the fellowship of the Holy Spirit be with us now and for evermore. Amen

Notes

1. The first exercise at the beginning of the session should be fun as well as making a serious point. Stress that people want all sorts of different things from life so there is no one answer.

2. The Grace in the *Prayer time* may not be familiar to people. Be prepared to have it written out so that all can join in.

5. What can I make of suffering?

AIM

The aim of this session is to help people explore their questions about the place of suffering in their lives and how it relates to belief in a God of love.

ABOUT OURSELVES

One of the team should tell the story of their own experience of coping with a painful situation. This need not be a story of physical suffering but must include the questions that were raised for him or her through the experience. This story should *not* contain an account of what helped the person to cope. A simple outline of the situation and of the questions raised is enough at this stage.

What questions do the group have about this part of our experience of life? (If the group is too big to make sharing these questions comfortable, divide into smaller units and come back together with the questions.)

List these for all to see.

INPUT 1

This might include:

(a)   We do not have 'the answer' to the problem of suffering. We do have a number of clues about it.

(b)   God does not send suffering as a punishment for sin. (We do, however, sometimes bring suffering on ourselves by our foolish actions.)

(c)   God will use suffering (he does not 'send' it) because he seeks to bring good out of pain.

(d)   We sometimes see later that we have grown as a person because we have been through an experience which caused us pain at the time.

(e)   Jesus provides us with an awareness that, when we suffer, God knows what we are going through. He is not remote from our suffering but has been there before us.

INPUT 2

The team member who told the story at the start of the session should now speak about what helped him or her through the experience. What did he or she do? Who helped and how? When and how did he or she experience God's presence?

GROUP WORK

Discuss:

Can suffering be of positive value in our lives and, if so, how? (Encourage people to share their own stories if they feel comfortable doing so.)

PRAYER TIME

Place a large crucifix in the centre of the group for all to see. Read Matthew 26:36–40 (The Garden of Gethsemane).

Invite people to offer their own 'heartbreaks' to God knowing that he has been there before them.

Pass the crucifix around the group, inviting each person to make a silent prayer of thanksgiving for the love of God seen in the suffering of Jesus, as they hold the cross in their hands.

A suitable hymn may be sung during this time (e.g. 'My song is love unknown', or 'When I survey the wondrous cross').

Notes

1. This session is bound to raise many deeply personal questions and needs to be handled with great sensitivity throughout. Be aware of the fact that some people may be in the middle of difficult or painful situations.
2. Do not put people into a position in which they feel they must reveal information about themselves when they are not ready to do so.
3. If you have a large group make sure smaller units are formed for more intimate sharing.

6. How is it possible to believe in God and in science?

AIM

To help people see that the question 'Is it true?' is not the same as 'Did it happen?' and that science and religion are not incompatible.

ABOUT OURSELVES

Story 1
One member of the team should tell the story of the 'Ugly Duckling'. (There is room for great fun here. It may be possible to act it out – certainly make it enjoyable.)
Ask the group:
'Did the story happen this way?'
'Is the story true?'

Story 2
A different member of the team should tell the following story. If possible, a story from their own experience would be preferable but, if not, the story quoted would suffice. Whatever story is used, it needs to be one which proclaims a truth but which did not happen exactly as portrayed.

I have a minor speech defect. I roll my 'r's. A slight affliction that would scarcely be worth comment except for the name I inherited from my parents. I remember when I was quite little, six or seven I think, I went to the Junior Library for the first time. A vast universe of knowledge was opening up before me. I was entering a new world of encyclopaedias and pop-up picture books. An exciting moment in a little boy's life. I handed the librarian the card I had been given at school. 'And what's your name?' she asked sweetly. 'John Ryan,' I responded eagerly. 'Lyons,' she repeated erroneously and ran through her card index. Perplexed, she turned back. 'What did you say your name was?' 'John Ryan,' I replied uncertainly. 'Riley,' she affirmed apologetically and . . . drew a second blank. A queue had now formed. Firmness entered her voice as she repeated her question. Colour rose in my cheeks as I stammered my replies. 'Nylon?' she queried. 'Iron?' she ventured. By now I was bright crimson, tears were forming in the corners of my eyes and the queue was getting agitated.'Could you spell it?' she asked to break the deadlock. I sniffled through the response: 'R. . .Y. . .A. . .N.' 'Ryan,' she exclaimed, 'why didn't you say that?' And she gave me a look, the sort of look we reserve for the demented. I didn't want the library tickets. I didn't want to enter the world of knowledge or go into the library ever again. I knew, how I knew, that the world is a wicked, horrible place, and worse, I knew that I was imperfect, inadequate. I couldn't even talk properly.

(Adapted from Christine Dodd, *Making Scripture Work*.)

Ask the group:

(a) Did this incident happen exactly as the author remembers it?

   (Draw out the fact that something like it did happen but that if a video were shown of the incident it would look very different from this account. The young boy faced many experiences such as this in his early life and this story contains the distilled essence of many such incidents.)

(b) Is the story true?

   (Draw out the fact that the story is profoundly true, for it speaks to everyone who has been publicly made aware of their imperfections, and it speaks about what it means to lose one's dignity.)

INPUT

From the stories draw out:

(a) Truth is a wider concept than 'Did it happen?'
(b) Some aspects of our faith can only be told in story form.
   (If we want to explain the meaning of a word such as 'courage' we do not give a dictionary definition, we tell a story – therefore this is the way we normally express truth.)
(c) There are some questions science cannot answer. It answers the 'How did things happen?' question. It does not set out to answer the 'What is truth?' question.

Story 3

Use a biblical story such as the Creation stories, Adam and Eve or Jonah. Ask the same questions as above.

   'Did it happen this way?'

   'Is it true?'

Help people to understand the distinction between these two and that science and religion are not incompatible.

PRAYER TIME

If possible use slides or pictures of Creation as a basis for prayer. Use one of the Creation psalms, e.g. Psalm 8, to go with this. If slides are not available, use a large poster.

Notes

1. Notice that this theme raises the tricky question of 'What is truth?' in relation to the Bible. It is important this is thoroughly explored. The use of Scripture is often hampered because people have not thought this question through for themselves.
2. Notice the use of humour and enjoyment in Story 2.
3. Notice the use of the visual in the *Prayer time*.

7. What can we make of a mystery?

AIM

To introduce people to the idea of mystery as a positive concept.

ABOUT OURSELVES

Ask people to jot down on a piece of paper their completion of the statement 'To me religion is . . .'

When everyone has had a chance to do this gather these together on a flip-chart.

INPUT

This might contain:

(a) Some common ideas about religion (you may be able to use cartoons on an overhead projector or large pictures for this). Include ideas such as
'Religion is against everything.'
'Religion is escape.'
'Religion is convention.'
'Religion is rubbish.'
'Religion is irrelevant.'
(b) Explain the true meaning of the word 'religion'. Religion seeks to answer life's questions:
'Why am I here?'
'Who am I?'
'What meaning has life?'
(c) Explain that these questions are answered in part but not in full. They remain a mystery.
(d) Explain what the word 'mystery' means. It is not something unintelligible or puzzling. We can never understand it completely.

(e)   Religion attempts to explore questions – it does not claim to give all the answers to everything. Religion means entering into mystery.

GROUP WORK

In groups, discuss these questions:
'What do you think religion is for?'
'In what ways are you a mystery to yourself?'
'How could religion help you enter into the mystery of life?'
Draw these together by requesting each group to give one joint answer to each of the questions. Draw out common themes.

PRAYER TIME

Have a large candle with an open Bible on a table. Allow a period of silence with the lit candle and perhaps some background music. Encourage people to reflect on what they have heard.

Close with the Lord's Prayer.

Notes

1. Notice the use of individuals' responses in *About ourselves*. Before you use the 'pencil-and-paper' technique make sure everyone can read and write. If you are unsure, 'brainstorm' verbally.
2. Notice the use of cartoons – make sure this is light-hearted but does not criticize those who honestly believe religion is irrelevant or merely convention.
3. Notice the use of music in the *Prayer time*.

8. How does God call me?

AIM

To enable participants to discover that God calls each one on the journey of faith and that the call comes in different ways.

ABOUT OURSELVES

Divide into pairs. Ask one person to spend two minutes telling the other one an incident that has happened to him or her that week. It can be either joyful or sad. The second person must not interrupt or comment. Change over, and repeat the process, with the second person telling a story from their experience for two minutes. Allow two minutes for both people to ask questions of the other and discuss.

In the whole group discuss what happened. Draw out:

the importance of listening
the importance of empathy
the importance of asking questions and discussion

INPUT

Read Luke 24:13–35 (every person should have a copy).

Divide the group into two. Arrange the chairs so that they are facing one another. One group should think of themselves as the disciples and look at the story from their point of view. The other group should try to see it from the point of view of Jesus. One member of the team should stand or sit between the two groups and go through the story verse by verse with them, asking questions to draw out how both parties felt. Pertinent questions should be asked such as 'How did you react when Jesus said that?', 'What did you think when the disciples seemed so despondent?', etc. The leader should not give his or her own point of view but elicit what was happening between the two parties.

After this draw out the following points:

(a)   Jesus walks with us no matter where we are going or how we feel.
(b)   Jesus listens to our stories.
(c)   Jesus gradually calls us to new understanding.
(d)   Jesus makes himself known to us through 'ordinary' things (i.e. the disciples recognized him because they had seen him break bread before and he used recognizable means of making himself known).
(e)   Jesus stays with them on their journey.

Stress the fact that God's call to journey in faith does not usually come in extraordinary ways but through everyday people and events.

GROUP WORK

In small groups, allow people to discuss how this model of the call of Jesus to the disciples to follow him reflects in their own lives.

> When have they been aware of Jesus *walking* with them?
>
> When have they known that he *listens* (perhaps through other people).
>
> When have incidents in their lives brought them to *new understanding*?
>
> What *ordinary things* have spoken to them of God?
>
> How is Jesus *calling* them on their journey now?

PRAYER TIME

Use a Bible and a bread roll as a focal point. You can also have a lighted candle if you wish.

Allow a time of quiet reflection.

Sing: 'Lead us, heavenly Father, lead us' or another suitable 'journey' hymn.

Prayer:

> Father, you walk with us on our journey through life and call us to faith in you.
>
> Stay with us and help us to be open to hear your voice and see your presence all around us. Through Jesus Christ our Lord. Amen.

Notes

1. Notice the blend of Scripture story and life story in the session.
2. Notice the way Scripture is used. It is designed to help people enter into the text in a new way and to 'experience' it as well as think about it. Care must be taken to avoid reading into the story elements that are not there.
3. Notice the use of the focal point in the *Prayer time*. This use of the visual as a symbol is important. Note also the use of silence in this closing part of the meeting.

Chapter 3

TRAVELLING WITH GOD

Mary did not come from a practising Christian family. She came into contact with the local church in a rather unusual way. Her daily journey to work began with a short walk to the bus stop. This was situated just outside the church building. Her presence there usually coincided with the end of morning Mass and so she frequently saw the same people emerging from the church. They had smiled and the smiles had turned to 'good mornings' and the 'good mornings' to short conversations about the weather or the state of the world in general. On really wet days she used to shelter in the porch. Eventually, curiosity got the better of her and she stepped inside.

She was surprised at what she found. Later she would say that it was all very strange and yet somehow comfortable and homely. 'It felt like I belonged there. I got used to going a bit early and spending time just sitting soaking up a bit of peace and quiet.' The question 'why' nagged at her. Why did she feel so at home there? Why were the people so respectful, leaving her alone when she needed it, but pleasant and sociable when they spoke? Why did they seem so contented and why on earth did they get up an hour before they needed in the mornings in order to go to Mass? What on earth was that all about anyway?

Mary had also started reading some of the leaflets and booklets at the back of church. They answered some of her questions and, rather to her surprise, made sense. But there were many more things she wanted to know about. What was this God Christians believed in like? How could anyone know? Who was Jesus and why did these poeple think his life had anything to do with today?

The poster she saw on the notice-board about the forthcoming meetings to be held in the parish seemed to hold out the possibility of finding some answers. But Mary knew no one and, although she was an independent and confident young woman, walking into a strange group in a strange place would take more courage than she felt she had. Perhaps one of the early-morning Mass attenders could help. She somewhat nervously approached the woman she spoke to most frequently. Yes, of course she could attend and, yes, it would be dealing with basic questions. No, the lady herself was not going but, if Mary would like to wait a bit, she would see if anyone else at Mass that morning was going. And so it was that Mary met Ruth. Together they went to the first sessions and, as Mary settled in, the questions began to tumble out. 'I wanted some answers', she said later. 'I wanted to know the basics about God and Jesus and what it could all mean for my life. I also wanted to see how other people thought and what had happened in their lives. I learnt a great deal through them as well as through all the information we were given. Both things were important. As I listened to their stories and told my own I began to see how God had been with me all along and how the Church's teaching about his relationship with us made so much sense.'

This chapter offers sessions on some of the basic questions people ask about the Christian faith. As is the case with all the material in this book you must decide for yourself when, where and how to use it. Choose the sessions carefully. You will find that some topics are dealt with in different ways in different sessions. For instance, there are two sessions on 'Who is Jesus?' You are unlikely to need both as there is a great deal of common material. When choosing which sessions to use look at the people you have, before you look at the material. Knowing them will help you assess what to discard and what to keep. Then, as always, adapt and adapt your chosen session until it is tailor-made for the specific needs of your group.

Included in this chapter is material for sessions on:

Whose world is it anyway?
How can I know God exists?
What are the Scriptures?
Why bother with the Bible?
What has God been doing all these years?
What is God like?
Can we trust the Gospels to tell us about Jesus?
What do I think about Jesus?
Who is Jesus? (2 sessions)
What does Jesus show us about God?
What happened to the people Jesus met?
What did Jesus teach?

How can I respond to Jesus?
How can I cope with failure?
How can I know I am forgiven?
What happens when I die?
Who is the Holy Spirit?

1. Whose world is it anyway?

AIM

The aim of this session is to enable people to explore their Christian understanding of God as a loving creator in a world where suffering exists.

Divide the group into two (if necessary you can sub-divide within these two groups into smaller units).

Ask one group to discuss and list all the things that point towards the existence of God as a loving creator.

Ask the other group to discuss and list all the things they think point towards a view that God does not exist.

Once this task has been completed, arrange the room so that the two groups, i.e. the 'prosecution' and the 'defence', are facing each other, with a table at one end facing both groups. At the table should sit the 'clerk of the court' (this person is really the facilitator, who keeps things running smoothly). To one side of him or her sits the 'Counsel for the Prosecution' and on the other side the 'Counsel for the Defence'. These two people should both be members of the RCIA team or people able to present an input in a clear manner.

Ask a spokesperson from each of the two groups to present their findings. This should be done without comment from the other group. No interruptions, questions or discussion are allowed! At the end of the presentation the Counsel for the Prosecution and the Counsel for the Defence should sum up their 'case'. The Clerk of the Court then draws out the salient points from each case. No judgement should be made or given.

If you wish you can extend this process and deepen it by allowing the Counsels for Prosecution and Defence to call witnesses from the two groups, i.e. they may call someone who has made a particular point in the group discussion to present that point. If this is done no cross-examination should be allowed.

It is a good idea at this point to have a break, perhaps for coffee or tea, to allow people to 'de-role' and to re-arrange the seating. This should be put into the normal seating positions where everyone can see and hear comfortably.

INPUT

A short input can now be given on the place of faith in the life of the Christian. It is important to point out that we are not asked to have faith in the untenable, nor are we faced with definitive and absolute proof of God's existence. Expand here on the importance of faith and God's desire for his children to be able to respond to him *in freedom*. This opens the way for people to believe or not to believe, but it also opens the way for a response to God which is one of loving faith.

PRAYER TIME

Read Genesis 1:1–2:3. It might be helpful to play some quiet background music whilst this is being read or to use slides or pictures as the reading progresses.

Close by saying together Psalm 8. (This will need to be provided for people either on an overhead projector or in written form.)

Notes

1. Notice the need for very careful planning for this session. This, of course, is the case for all sessions but in this particular instance it is doubly important. This way of working may well raise doubts in people's minds so it is important that the whole session is handled with extreme care and sensitivity.
2. Notice the importance of the 'Counsel for the Prosecution' and the 'Counsel for the Defence'. These people really must be able to present a coherent case and it is important that one is not 'better' than the other due to presentation. It is a good idea if they get together first and decide how they will present it and perhaps even write out their presentation, bearing in mind that this may need to be altered in the light of what the groups produce.
3. Notice that no 'judgement' is to be given here. The important point is to open up for people the awareness that belief in God is about faith *and* that this faith is not in conflict with our abilities to make intellectual decisions based on what we see, hear and experience.

4. Notice the break between the end of the 'courtroom scene' and the *Input*. This allows people to chat to each other and to 'de-role'.

Members of the team should be aware that there may be people who need to talk to them individually after this session.

2. How can I know God exists?

AIM

To help people think through their own reasons for believing in God.

ABOUT OURSELVES

Allow people to chat to each other in pairs as to why they think God exists and why they think he does not exist.

Two people from the RCIA team should present their own stories of why they believe God exists. This should contain *personal experience* rather than a theological treatise. Allow people to chat in the same pairs to see how the two stories relate to their own.

INPUT

This should cover:

(a) what we mean by natural revelation (i.e. God revealing himself through the natural world);
(b) what we mean by revelation (i.e. God revealing himself through the Scriptures and the Church);
(c) what we mean by personal experience.

GROUP WORK

In groups of five or six look at the three areas (natural revelation, revelation and personal experience) and share how you have experienced any of these.

PRAYER TIME

Place an opened Bible and an article from the created world (e.g. a vase of flowers, piece of driftwood or a stone) on a table, along with a calendar opened at the appropriate month.

Pray together the following prayer (you will need copies for everyone).

God of goodness and love,
we thank you that you make yourself known to us
in the world around us,
in the way you lead us through our lives
and in the story of your love throughout history.
May our eyes always be open to see you around us
that we may come closer to you as we journey onwards.
We ask this through Jesus Christ our Lord.
Amen.

Notes

1. Notice the use of personal experience in this session, in particular the importance of the sharing of stories by the RCIA team.
2. Notice in the *Input* the use of technical words like 'natural revelation'. It is vital that people understand what these terms mean. All too often we use technical theological words assuming that people understand their meaning when often this is not the case. Be very careful about the use of language.

3. What are the Scriptures?

AIM

The aim of this session is to introduce people to Scripture as the living word of God.

ABOUT OURSELVES

Ask people on their own to recall something really good, some incident in their lives when they were really happy. Ask them to think of a colour, image or word to associate with it.

Now ask them to think of something really awful, an incident they found difficult to cope with. Again, recall an image, a colour or a word associated with this event. They do not have to share this with anyone.

Ask people now to call out a story of Jesus that they like, something that makes them feel good and joyful and happy. List these.

Then ask them to call out a story of Jesus they dislike. Again list these.

INPUT 1

Explain:

(a)   The Scriptures are *stories of God*. They tell us who, what, where, how and when things about God. They do not give us *the* picture but many pictures of God. This richness is necessary. We look to the Scriptures as a source for our understanding of God.

(b)   The Scriptures are *stories about ourselves*. They tell us who we are, and how we fit in with God. All human life is here – joy, sorrow, pain, grief, anger, frustration. There is the richness of human experience. We look to the Scriptures as a source' of our response to God. This is why the Bible is important for today. It speaks about the God of the present as well as the past. It speaks of our stories of the present as well as the stories of others who had faith in God in the past.

INPUT 2

Ask people to shout out anything they know from the Scriptures. List these into areas, e.g. history (from a biased viewpoint since the authors were not interested in objective history), story, poetry, laws, etc. Explain that the Bible is a library, not one book.

INPUT 3

Talk about how the Bible came to be written down.

(a)   A community seeking God had experiences of life and people and events. (Link this with the idea that being in the RCIA group means that we collect together stories and experiences of our life together. If we wanted future groups to know what we did we would write this down.)

(b)   As they looked back and shared their memory and reflected on these experiences the community could see what God was doing through them.

(c)   The prophets and preachers and teachers had proclaimed God's doings. These needed to be recorded.

(d)   To ensure that future generations would hear the story accurately, people began to write down what had happened and the experiences of the community, the proclamations. They did this as a way of praising and thanking God and celebrating his loving care. The *pro-*

clamation was first. The *writing down* came later. When anyone read the written text, he/she would refer to the community for help in understanding it – because it is the community's story. He/she would ask God for understanding – because it is the story of God's doings in the community. So reading the Bible *and* seeking understanding in prayer and community still go hand in hand.

IN SMALL GROUPS

What I would like to know about the Bible is .... ?
Allow time for these questions to be given back and answered.

PRAYER TIME

Have a Bible open as a focal point. Read Nehemiah 2–3, 5–6 and 9.

Notes

1. Notice the fairly lengthy *Input*. This is necessary in this session.
2. Notice the emphasis on Scripture as a record of the past *and* of strength for today.

4. Why bother with the Bible?

AIM

To help people to think of the Bible as the living word of God.

ABOUT OURSELVES

Begin the session with a time of silent prayer and quiet reflection. Ask people to concentrate on any story about Jesus' dealings with people and to try and imagine him in that situation. If necessary give some examples, e.g. Zacchaeus, Jairus' daughter, blind Bartimeus, etc. Close this time of reflection with a prayer asking for God's guidance that we might hear him speaking to us through his word and through each other.

BIBLE WORK

If necessary divide the group into smaller units of about six people.

1. One member reads the following passage (Luke 5:12–16) slowly.

    Once, when he was in one of the cities, there was a man covered with leprosy. When he saw Jesus, he bowed with his face to the ground, and begged him, 'Lord, if you choose, you can make me clean.' Then Jesus stretched out his hand, touched him, and said, 'I do choose. Be made clean.' Immediately the leprosy left him. And he ordered him to tell no one. 'Go,' he said, 'and show yourself to the priest, and, as Moses commanded, make an offering for your cleansing, for a testimony to them.' But now more than ever the word about Jesus spread abroad; many crowds would gather to hear him and to be cured of their diseases. But he would withdraw to deserted places and pray.

2. Make sure that everyone has a copy of this text. Ask people to read it again for themselves in silence. Suggest that they pick out one phrase or word that stands out for them (e.g. 'touched him').
    Each person reads out their phrase or word. There must be *no* discussion.

3. Next encourage people to share *why* each one chose the phrase or word. Other people in the group should listen carefully and only when all who wish to do so have contributed should discussion be allowed.

4. At the close of this exercise suggest that the group pray together in the light of the passage both for themselves and for others.

INPUT

This should contain:

(a) the Church's understanding of the Bible as the living word of God (a record of the story of our faith, the story of God's dealings with his people, the way in which God communicates with us today).

(b) the Bible as food for our journey (a means through which we hear God).

(c) the Bible as a guide for our lives (beware of giving the impression the Bible answers all questions!).

This input should be preceded by some feedback from the groups as to how they found the experience of working with the given Bible passage.

No closing liturgy is given for this session as the *group work* was in itself an experience of prayer.

Notes

1. Notice the way in which the group was encouraged to pray together as well as to discuss.
2. Notice in the *Input* the relationship between the Bible as a record of how God has dealt with his people in the past *and* a means of communicating with us today.

5. What has God been doing all these years?

AIM

To help participants see the relevance of the Old Testament and clear up misconceptions regarding it.

ABOUT OURSELVES

In the whole group brainstorm *all* the Old Testament stories, events and passages that people can remember. (Be prepared for people to know very little.) Make a list for all to see.

INPUT

(a) Draw out from the list how the story of revelation shows (among other things) that God:
   creates,
   sustains,
   calls,
   judges,
   forgives,
   stays with his people.
(b) Explain that the Old Testament is made up of different *types* of literature to express this, i.e. story, poetry, laws, parable, proverbs, etc.
(c) Explain why the Old Testament is important. The God portrayed here is not a different God from the one portrayed by the New Testament. Throughout the Bible it is the same God who creates, sustains, calls, judges, forgives and stays with his people. The God revealed in the Old Testament is also the God of Jesus. (It is important at this

point to clear up any misunderstandings about the God of the Old Testament being a vengeful or vicious God.)

GROUP WORK

Discuss what Old Testament story has a message for you and why.
    What question do you want to ask about the Old Testament?
    (Allow time for people to express their questions and for some response to be made.)

PRAYER TIME

Use the story of Abraham setting out from Ur (Genesis 12) as a basis for prayer.

Notes

1. There may well be a considerable amount of misunderstanding or ignorance about the place of the Old Testament in the life of the Church. (For further clarification on the Church's teaching see the Council document of Vatican II, *Dei Verbum*.)
2. Press home the point that we should not think of the God of Jesus 'superseding' the God of the Former Covenant. It is the same God.

6. What is God like?

AIM

The aim of this session is to use an Old Testament story which reveals to us what God is like and what this means for today.

ABOUT OURSELVES

One member of the RCIA team should tell the story of a real-life incident where he or she felt totally 'at sea'. This need not be anything major but it should be emotionally important. The person should tell the facts of the case but also speak about the effect it had on him or her and how the situation was resolved. Ask people in pairs to share very briefly a similar incident in their own lives. (This may be omitted if you prefer.)

INPUT

Use the story of the Exodus. Since this is far too long to read, it could be 'acted out' or role-played by the team members, or simply told as a story. However it is done, the account should include the following:

slavery in Egypt
liberation
wandering in the wilderness
being hungry for food
turning away from God
looking towards the promised land

Draw out these points from the story. It is best to write them down on a flip-chart or overhead projector. Opposite the list write down what this tells us about God and ourselves. This should include:

There are times when we feel enslaved:
God *liberates* us.
There are times when we wander in the wilderness:
God *guides* us.
There are times when we are hungry and thirsty:
God *feeds* us.
There are times when we turn away from God:
God *forgives* us.
There are times when we look in hope to the future:
God *walks* with us to the promised land.

GROUP WORK

Use the *Journey in Faith* illustration, on page 45, as the basis of a worksheet for people to work with on their own. If time allows and if they wish, it can be shared together in small groups or pairs.

In the group work allow time for questions and response to the exercise. What did people learn about God?

PRAYER TIME

Psalm 107:1–9 as the basis for the Liturgy.

JOURNEY IN FAITH

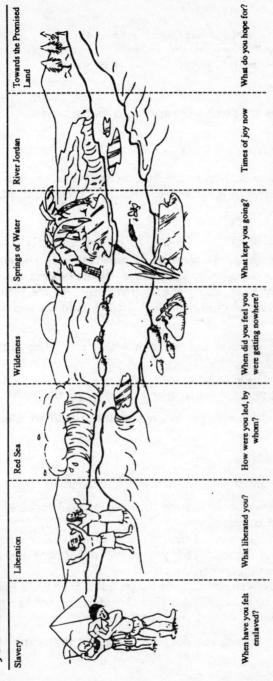

Slavery	Liberation	Red Sea	Wilderness	Springs of Water	River Jordan	Towards the Promised Land
When have you felt enslaved?	What liberated you?	How were you led, by whom?	When did you feel you were getting nowhere?	What kept you going?	Times of joy now	What do you hope for?

From *Telling the Story, Sharing the Faith* (Home Mission Committee of the General Synod Board of Mission and Unity).

Notes

1. Notice the use of individual work in this session.
2. Notice the link between the Scripture story, the explanation of what it means and the way it relates to life today.

7. Can we trust the Gospels to tell us about Jesus?

AIM

The aim of this session is to introduce people to the Gospels and their stories of Jesus and to clear up any misconceptions regarding them.

ABOUT OURSELVES

Use a set of about six pictures. If possible these should be slides, but not necessarily. The pictures should be of one event, e.g. a holiday or an important Church event. All the pictures should therefore be of one incident. Use them in the following ways:

(a)   Arrange them in the order in which they were *actually taken*.
(b)   Rearrange the order *to tell a story*.
(c)   Rearrange the order to *make a particular point*.

The point of the exercise is to use pictures in a different order for a different reason.

INPUT

This should contain an explanation of the fact that

(a)   the Gospels were written to make particular points for different communities;
(b)   the authors arranged their material to suit their purposes (therefore the story each gospel tells is not necessarily in chronological order);
(c)   the authors sometimes left things out if they were not of interest to their audience (i.e. they do not intend to give a complete historical and biographical summary).

Stress the fact that all this does not mean that the Gospels are untrue!

An alternative way of making the same points

ABOUT OURSELVES

1. Two or three team members could act out a short playlet. It should last only three or four minutes. It does not really matter what the play contains as long as it has movement, different incidents happening within it, various comings and goings.
2. Ask one other team member sitting in the audience to give an account of what the play was about.
3. Ask the wider group if they think it is a true record. Ask what would they like to add or leave out.
4. Ask the group how they would tell the story to:

(a) a group of children;
(b) a friend from another country.

The point of the exercise is to draw out that stories are adapted for the audience for which they are being recorded, and that no one person records things in exactly the same way. Link this to the Gospels. You may need to talk about the distinction between 'is it true?' and 'did it happen?' Because something did not happen exactly as recorded does not mean there is no truth in it. (See chapter 2, page 26.)

Give a summary of the differences between the four Gospels. Explain that the Church developed its understanding of who Jesus was as time went on. We have a record of this in the Letters of Paul and the early Church writings.

GROUP WORK

Ask people to choose their favourite Gospel story and share with each other why it is their favourite. What does this say about Jesus?

PRAYER TIME

Place a Bible in a position of honour open at the New Testament. Read Luke 4:16–20. Use a prayer thanking God for the revelation made known to us in the Scriptures.

Notes

1. Be prepared for some questions of the 'Did it really happen as it is written?' variety. Be sensitive when tackling this.
2. Stress the importance of the Gospels as the *living* word of God for today; God's way of revealing himself.

8. What do I think about Jesus?

AIM

This session aims to help participants see the link between Jesus and the Old Testament and to give an introduction to the understanding of Jesus as revelation of the Father. Give out the 'Images of Jesus' sheets. Ask people to circle six images which speak to them. Ask them to think about

What do their words tell them about their picture of who Jesus is? (See the questions on the sheet below).

IMAGES OF JESUS

Look at the following list of words and images associated with Jesus. Circle six which you think best describe who Jesus is for you.

Healer	Rock	New Man
Friend	Shepherd	Creator
Redeemer	Logos	Servant
Saviour	Lover	Lamb
Lord	Gentle	Mild
Vine	Meek	Christ
Door	Master	Son of Man
Fool	Helper	Light
Prophet	Brother	Healer
Herald	Leader	Son of God
Revolutionary	Refuge	Other ....
		....

What do your words tell you about your picture of Jesus?
Is he more human or divine for you?
Is he close or far away from you?
Is he strong or gentle or both for you?

(Adapted from Anne Bishop and Eldon Hay, *Telling My Story, Sharing My Faith*, United Church of Canada.)

Share your ideas in pairs or threes.

ABOUT OURSELVES

Use the story of the woman with a haemorrhage and Jairus' daughter (Luke 8:40–56).

1. In small groups ask people to draw out from this passage what it tells us about Jesus.
2. Ask each group to write these findings down on large sheets of paper. Put these up somewhere where all can see and make a master list of what this passage tells us about Jesus.

INPUT

From this draw out the following:

(a) Jesus *called* people to him. (He was welcomed by the crowd. He obviously attracted their interest.)
(b) He *responds* to our cries for help. He is in control of what is happening around him.
(c) He *respects* the dignity of others.
(d) He *forgives* and heals.
(e) He is a *human being* with feelings. (He is ridiculed by the crowd.) Stress he is not God 'playing' at being a human.
(f) He has *power* to alter the seemingly unalterable. Some input should be given here on the understanding of Jesus as both God and man.

GROUP WORK

Look again at your *Images of Jesus* sheet.

(a) Would you like to change or add any other images in the light of what you have learned?
(b) What do you think it means *for us* that Jesus was truly human and truly divine?

PRAYER TIME

Use the same story in an imaginative prayer exercise. This means reading the story slowly and then encouraging people to enter into it themselves and imagine they are there. How is Jesus calling them? How do they respond?

Notes

1. Notice the way the *Images of Jesus* sheet is used again at the end of the session as a way of helping people reflect on what they have discovered.
2. Notice the use of imaginative prayer in the Liturgy. Be sensitive to how much silence people can comfortably manage and be aware that this form of prayer may not be for everyone.

9. Who is Jesus? (1)

AIM

The aim of this session is to help people discover some of the Church's teaching about the person and mission of Jesus.

Begin the session by reading Mark 8:27.

ABOUT OURSELVES

Have ten or more 'pictures' of Jesus around the room for people to look at. These could be reproductions from Old Masters, stills from biblical films and modern-day pictures. Try to make sure they are varied in style and in content.

Ask people to look at the pictures and to choose which one they like best. In small groups share why the picture was chosen and what it is about the picture that makes it 'speak'.

Come together and share in the wider group what the pictures tell us about Jesus.

INPUT

This should include four main aspects of the Church's teaching about Jesus.

(a) Jesus was an *historical figure*. He was a person of his time and lived in a particular time and place.
(b) Jesus was *truly human*. He was not God 'dressed up' as a human being but shared all our human feelings and experiences. (Use examples of this from the gospels, e.g. frustration with the authorities, loneliness in Gethsemane, grief over a death, etc.) Jesus was like us in everything, except sin. Jesus shows us what it means to be a perfect human.
(c) Jesus was *divine*. The Church teaches that God was in

Jesus. He shows us what God is like – the revelation of the Father. The expression of the vastness of God's love for us is seen in his Son Jesus who comes among us and is willing to go through death to show the extent of God's love.

(d) Jesus is *present now*. He is not a figure of history but a living presence among us. His resurrection is a message not only of victory over death but of the fact of his life with us now.

GROUP WORK

Discuss: Jesus came from the Father, lived as a human being and his Spirit now dwells within his followers.

What does this tell us about God and his relationship with us?

PRAYER TIME

Use one of the pictures of Jesus as a focal point.

Four people should read the following sentences, allowing time between each one.

'Jesus said, "Peace I leave with you, my peace I give to you".'
Let us ask God to give us his peace.

'Jesus said, "I am the good shepherd. The good shepherd lays down his life for his sheep".'
Let us thank God that Christ came to show us his love.

'Jesus said, "I have come that you may have life and have it in all its fullness".'
Let us ask God to give us his life within us.

Notes

1. Notice here that the relationship between Father, Son and Spirit is mentioned but not specifically covered. You may need to discuss the concept of the Trinity.
2. Notice the use of pictures in this session. The visual is important and provides a way of helping people articulate their images of Jesus.

10. Who is Jesus? (2)

AIM

This session offers a different way of covering similar ground to the previous one and has similar aims.

Examine the following statements about Jesus. Circle the 'Yes' or 'No' after each, then discuss the results. The *input* should spend time on the apparently difficult areas of Christ-ology.

Is it true that Jesus:

Was a good man, but little more than that?	Yes/No
Was God just seeming to be human?	Yes/No
Was a circumcised Jew?	Yes/No
Knew everything about everything from infancy?	Yes/No
Was not able to sin?	Yes/No
Is related to all of us?	Yes/No
Offers us a life of pleasure?	Yes/No
Prefers some people to others?	Yes/No
Affects our lives only after death?	Yes/No
Performed miracles as signs that God's kingdom had come?	Yes/No
Rewards only those who have deserved it?	Yes/No
Is living, loving and active now?	Yes/No

In twos, think about this question: if you had to describe Jesus to a Martian, what would you choose to say about him? Write down your ideas in just one or two sentences, then tell your partner. Explain any words which a Martian with poor English would find difficult.

PRAYER TIME

At the end of a suitable period of silence conclude with every-one saying the Our Father.

(Adapted from Deborah M. Jones, *Focus on Faith*, Kevin Mayhew.)

11. What does Jesus show us about God?

AIM

To use the Bible story of the Exodus to help people understand Jesus as Revelation of the Father.

(This session can be used in conjunction with the session *What is God like?*)

INPUT

Introduce or recall the basic story of the Exodus. The elements of this story should be listed so that all can see. It should include:

(a) the people were enslaved;
(b) they were liberated;
(c) they wandered in the wilderness;
(d) they were hungry;
(e) they turned away from God;
(f) they looked towards the promised land.

Outline the picture of God that this story gives.

(a) He calls one of his own (Moses) while they are still slaves in Egypt.
(b) He liberates them and sets them free.
(c) He guides them in the wilderness.
(d) He feeds them.
(e) He forgives them.
(f) He offers them a new beginning.

Explain that Jesus has not *replaced* the Old Testament but *fulfilled* it. By looking at Jesus we can see what God is really like. Jesus reveals the Father in the fullest sense.

Look at the list again.

(a) • Jesus is one who is like us (just as Moses was one of the Hebrews).
     • Jesus is truly human, not God dressed up pretending to be human.
     • Jesus is what we should be – what God wants us to be.
(b) Jesus *sets us free* just as God liberated the Hebrews. Jesus shows us a God who wants us to be free. We are all crippled in some way or other, we are all enslaved.
(c) Jesus shows us a God who *guides us* (just as God guided the people in the wilderness). There are times when we

are not sure where we are going. The people in the wilderness learned that God guided them and was always with them. Jesus shows us a God who guides and is always with us though we do not always recognize him (compare the Emmaus story – Luke 24).

(d) Jesus shows us a God who *feeds us*. The Israelites needed sustenance on the journey. Food was given to them in the form of manna. Jesus gives us new strength to continue our journey of faith. He feeds and strengthens us with word and sacrament on our journey.

(e) Jesus *forgives us* just as the Israelites were forgiven when they failed to follow God (i.e. the golden calf). God does this throughout history, always forgiving and recalling his people to a new beginning. Jesus shows us a God who continues to forgive us even to the extent of dying for us. The depth of God's love is shown in Jesus' crucifixion.

(f) Jesus shows us a God who *offers us new beginnings* (just as God offered people a new beginning in the Promised Land). The Israelites crossed over to a new beginning when they crossed the Jordan. Jesus offers us hope by showing us a God who continually offers us new beginnings, not just when we die but always. His life revealed the Father, offering to people a new start and a new way of life.

GROUP WORK

In small groups answer the following questions:

(a) Jesus came to show us what God the Father is like and how we can know him.
   What sort of person do *you* think Jesus was?

(b) What does he show *you* about God?

PRAYER TIME

Use an icon or picture of Jesus and allow people a time of quiet reflection so that they may respond to Jesus' revelation of the Father.

Notes

1. The lengthy *Input* of this session. Much of this can be done 'interactively', i.e. drawing points out from the group as you go along.
2. Notice the use of the visual in the *Prayer time*. This is important.

12. What happened to the people Jesus met?

AIM

The aim of this session is to give participants an awareness of the various ways people reacted to Jesus and what this means for their own relationship with him.

BRAINSTORM

Ask the group what they think Jesus was like. (You may do this by inviting people to call out or by splitting into small groups and then compiling a complete list of responses. Make sure the responses are written up clearly for all to see.)

INPUT 1

Draw out:

(a) Jesus had charisma that attracted people.
(b) Jesus spoke forthrightly, which sometimes upset people.
(c) Jesus' words and actions demanded a response – either positive or negative.

GROUP WORK

Split into threes or fours and give each group a Gospel passage. These passages are stories of people who met Jesus. Obvious examples are:

> Jairus (Luke 8:40–42, 49–56)
> Zacchaeus (Luke 19:1–10)
> The woman taken in adultery (John 8:1–11)
> Pilate (John 19:1–16)
> The woman with a haemorrhage (Luke 8:43–48)
> Nicodemus (John 3:1–12)
> Matthew (Matthew 9:9–13)
> The rich young man (Luke 18:18–26)

Ask the groups to discuss and respond to:

(a) How did Jesus react to the person concerned?
(b) What did meeting Jesus mean for the person concerned?
(c) What was it about Jesus that created the reaction? (Refer back to the first list the group made at the brainstorming session.)

Report the findings to the whole group.

INPUT 2

Draw out:

(a) Jesus' care for the dignity of each individual and his will-
     ingness to interact with them.
(b) Meeting Jesus demanded a response (either positive or
     negative). His person and presence required that people
     make the choice about him.
(c) Jesus is the same today. He challenges us to respond.

PRAYER TIME

Use one of the stories from the Gospels, which should be read
slowly and carefully. Leave a time for quiet prayer. Suggest
that people think about how they respond to the Jesus of the
Gospels.

   Close with a prayer of commitment.

Notes

1. Note the use of Scripture and the way in which people are encour-
    aged to explore it.
2. Note the link between the people Jesus met during his time on
    earth and the way in which his challenge comes to us today.

13. What did Jesus teach?

AIM

This session is designed to highlight only one instance of the
teaching of Jesus, i.e. the Beatitudes, and through this to enable
people to see some of the teaching of Jesus and its relevance
for today.

ABOUT OURSELVES

In pairs, ask people to talk about what would make them really
happy. (Use the term 'fulfilled' or 'truly contented' if this would
be better.)

INPUT

This might include:

(a) The concept of wholeness (link this to fulfilment) which Jesus wants for all his followers. He comes that we may have life in all its fullness.

(b) The concept of unity, as opposed to division and divisiveness. He prays that we may be one.

(c) The concept of 'all is not what it seems', i.e. the idea of paradox in the Beatitudes; the Kingdom given to the poor in spirit, the gentle inheriting the earth, the persecuted rejoicing, etc.

GROUP WORK

Give each group one (or at the most two) of the Beatitudes with which to work. Encourage them to tease out one instance of life today which illustrates Jesus' meaning. Draw these together in a full session.

PRAYER TIME

Use the Beatitudes as a basis for this. Each of the groups could read its Beatitude with silence between and perhaps an illustration from everyday life.

Notes

1. The *Input* here needs to be fairly lengthy and to express clearly the teaching of Jesus and its relevance for today.
2. Do not dismiss any ideas the group come up with in their interpretation of the Beatitudes for today. If necessary add to the interpretation and, if it is right off-beam, suggest a better way of looking at it. *Never* ignore or belittle what people have done.

14. How can I respond to Jesus?

AIM

The aim of this session is to help people see how Jesus continues to challenge us today. His presence enables us to respond to the implications of living the Christian life today.

ABOUT OURSELVES

Ask one person to read this passage aloud.

> The bus was full. I was sitting halfway down as it juddered to a halt. The doors opened and two or three people got off. Then on to the bus came a man whose face was very badly disfigured. The whole left-hand side of his head seemed about half an inch lower than the right-hand side. He was tall, well built and with the most beautiful hands I have ever seen. As he got on the bus and paid his fare the whole group went quiet. An embarrassed silence spread from the front to the back of the vehicle. Then one person right at the back said in a loud voice, 'He shouldn't be allowed out looking like that, upsetting the rest of us.' For one moment I saw the look on his face. It was a fleeting glimpse. He turned away. But in that moment I had seen the face of the suffering Christ. The woman next to me said his name was John and he lived just down her street. 'People always shun him', she said. 'He is a good and gentle man.' She paused. Then she got up, walked up to him, touched him on the shoulder. 'Hello, John', she said. 'Hello, Margaret.' And then she kissed him. He smiled. A wave of relief swept through the bus. The atmosphere that had been rent asunder was made whole.

Share in threes or fours how you felt as the story was read, particularly the action of the woman.

(a)   What connections are there between this story and the death and resurrection of Jesus?

(b)   Can you think of a time in your own life when a particular action transformed a situation from being deadly to being life-saving?

(c)   What can we learn from this story about being in a community of followers of Jesus today?

You may like to get some responses from the group but this is not strictly necessary.

INPUT

When the Christian community gather together there are many things we do.

(a)   *We remember* Jesus.
      We remember him in his pain and suffering.
      We remember he loved us so much that he gave every ounce of his living so that we might know that nothing can separate us from the love and forgiveness of God.

(b) *We commit ourselves.*
As his followers we commit ourselves to live our lives in his presence.
(c) *We remember others.*
We remember the people who are closest to us and those we meet everyday, and we consciously bring into the presence of God the situations in which we find ourselves.
(d) We *make connections* between what we know of Jesus and what he means to us and our daily lives. We begin to see things with the eyes of Jesus. We begin to see him in the things and the people around us. As we begin to see him, so we begin to co-operate with him.

GROUP WORK

In what ways do we see Jesus in the world in which we live? How can I co-operate with Jesus in my own situation?

PRAYER TIME

Allow people to become still. Suggest that they think of one person or event in their own lives where God has been very real to them. Use the prayer of thanksgiving. Close by saying the 'Glory Be' together.
(Adapted from *Towards Deeper Faith*, Catholic Adult Education Service, Archdiocese of Adelaide, Australia, 1985.)

15. How can I cope with failure?

AIM

The aim of this session is to explore an aspect of living we all experience and often find distressing: failure. We will look at Jesus' life and his fidelity in the face of failure and then look at our own experience of trying to be faithful today.

ABOUT OURSELVES 1

Here is a group of statements. (They will need to be typed out and circulated or read out by different people within the team.)

'This is the twentieth time I have gone for an interview and the twentieth time I haven't got the job.'

'How can I admit to my parents that I've failed in my marriage?'

'He'd been down for ages, nothing seemed to help. Then one morning he overdosed. I felt such a failure because I couldn't help him.'

'I look at my teenage children and ask what went wrong? They don't even speak to me about anything that really matters. I'm a complete failure to them.'

'Now I'm old and can't work, I'm not wanted by anyone. What's the point?'

'I'm no good, I'll never be as clever as my sister.'

'Coming home and telling my wife I'd been made redundant was like admitting the greatest failure. I can't even support her and the children.'

RESPONSES

Try to identify – for yourself, not for sharing – areas of failure in your life. In pairs share how feeling a failure affects a person and those around her or him.

Can you recall a time when what first seemed a failure became a positive experience for you? Where is God when you feel a failure?

INPUT 1

This might include:

Questions about failure:
(a) What causes it? (Was it poor judgement, lack of understanding or selfish sinfulness in the one who failed which caused the failure?)
What were the long-term results? Was it all loss or did it in fact lead to something better, something good?
(b) It is not always easy to see the positive side of failure when it happens but we can sometimes recognize it later on.
(c) God uses failure to help us in our own journey of faith. God never wastes anything.

ABOUT OURSELVES 2

Here are some statements about Jesus (as before, either you will need to have them written out to give to people or members of the team should read them out aloud).

'Do you also wish to go away?'

'My God, my God, why have you forsaken me?'

'When his family heard it, they went out to restrain him, for people were saying "He has gone out of his mind".'

'Are you also still without understanding?'

'Let him be crucified!'

'Have I been with you all this time, Philip, and you still do not know me?'

'When many of his disciples heard it they said, "This teaching is difficult; who can accept it?" '

'When they came to the place that is called the Skull, they crucified Jesus there with the criminals, one on his right and one on his left.'

'He came to what was his own, and his own people did not accept him.'

On your own try to identify – for yourself, not for sharing – which of these statements stands out for you. In pairs discuss: Was God distant from Jesus' suffering? From his death? What difference does knowing Jesus' experience make to our own experience of failure? How does God draw near to us in our sufferings or sense of failure?

INPUT 2

This should include:

(a) Jesus put his whole energy – in words and actions – into conveying what he knew gave meaning and purpose to life but even his closest friends did not understand. His failure was not due to any fault on his part; the message he brought was too strong for people to handle!

(b)   Jesus did not falter in his trust in the loving God. He remained faithful. His most apparent experience of failure, the crucifixion, became the central place where his message was made clear for the whole world.

(c)   God raised Jesus from the dead, thus affirming his message and confirming his trust. What appeared to be failure was transformed into new life. After the resurrection people seemed more able to grasp or be grasped by the truth Jesus had struggled to convey.

(d)   It is through the apparent failure of Jesus that people still know they are loved, forgiven, saved and freed to spread the knowledge of his love wherever they go.

GROUP WORK

Ask the group, if they can, either to compose a poem or to draw a picture or to produce a piece of drama showing the transformation of failure into new life, in the light of what they have learned.

PRAYER TIME

Have a crucifix as a focal point for this short time of prayer. Quietly read Psalm 22. Use a prayer asking that we may trust even where we fail.

(Adapted from *Towards Deeper Faith*, Catholic Adult Education Service, Archdiocese of Adelaide, Australia, 1985.)

16. How can I know I am forgiven?

AIM

The aim of this session is to explore the Christian understanding of the atoning work of Christ and its meaning for today.

INTRODUCTION

Explain that in this session we are going to introduce a small word with a big meaning: *Sin*. We shall also explore what can be done about it.

In the large group ask people to call out their responses to the statement 'I think sin is . . .'. (If you wish you can do this in smaller groups or in twos and threes, gathering responses together at the end.)

INPUT 1

Explain that sin is:

(a) not *only* doing wrong things (or not doing right ones): our activities, or lack of them, are symptoms of a basic deeper orientation;

(b) the result of our desire to 'do our own thing regardless of God';

(c) a 'missing the mark' or 'missing the target'.

Ask people to spend a moment reflecting in silence on their own particular 'problem area' in this regard. Stress this is a personal exercise only. They do not have to talk about it to anyone else. At the end of this you may wish to say together 'I confess . . .'

One of the team should now tell the following story:

A man was on his journey to Paradise. All his life he had been travelling towards it. Sometimes he was held up by rivers and landslides, sometimes he went the wrong way and needed a guide to put him back on the right path. By many devious and difficult paths he had travelled on. Now he could see his goal in the distance. The lush land, flowing with milk and honey, stretched out before him. But between that glorious land and his path lay an enormous chasm.

The man sat down and looked. He focused his mind on the glories of the One who awaited him and that kingdom of love and peace that he was about to enter. As he did so the chasm began to narrow. Then his mind wandered and he thought of all that would be his and the glorious possessions he would own once he had crossed into that land. As his thoughts wandered in this direction the chasm widened. How could he cross? He sat perplexed by the edge of the great canyon and wondered what to do.

At first he thought he would build a bridge. This bridge he thought should be one of prayer. If he prayed hard enough the chasm might reduce enough for him to jump over, so he tried earnestly to pray as hard as he could but, no matter how hard he tried, the gulf was too big for him. His next idea was to build a bridge made of good deeds. Busily he set about helping all who needed it. To the poor he gave money, to the sick he gave his time and his skill, but still the chasm remained. A third idea came to him. Perhaps the gap would narrow if he were truly repentant. So in sackcloth and eating no food he expressed his sorrow, but, although the canyon narrowed, still it was too great a gulf for him to cross. Despondently he sat down, at a loss as to what to do.

While he was sitting by the edge of the chasm he heard a noise from afar. The sound of trumpets came to him on the wind and he saw the sun glinting on the banners held aloft in a procession as it left the gates of the city in the far distance. It approached the other side of the canyon and then he saw a man in the centre. This man stepped to the edge of the gulf and called to him, 'What is it you desire?' 'Sir,' he replied, 'I desire to come to you, to your fair land, to find rest and refreshment and to discover life in all its fullness.' 'What is preventing you?' 'The chasm, sir. The more I think of myself and the more I do for my own satisfaciton the wider it gets but the more I think of you and the life offered to me, the narrower it becomes. Yet it is never narrow enough for me to cross. I have tried to build bridges but they are never long enough.' 'Do not worry', came the reply. While the man watched the chasm slowly began to close. It was almost complete but still it was too big for him to cross. Then the king lay down and stretching himself full length he reached across forming himself into a human bridge. And so the man managed to cross the chasm. He did so only because the king himself opened the way and made himself a life-giving channel.

GROUP WORK

Ask people to discuss in groups what they think this story has to say about sin, its effects and the way it is forgiven.

INPUT 2

Draw out:

(a)   Our sin does not stop God from loving us. No matter what we do he longs for us to be one with him.

(b)   Jesus came to make us at one with God (at-one-ment). This is what he wants us to be and the sort of relationship he wants us to have. The chasm between us and God is not of his making.

(c)   Jesus' death shows us the lengths to which God will go to make us at one with him.

(d)   Jesus' death is not God inflicting his anger for our sin on Jesus. It is not about punishment, it is about reconciliation.

(e)   We cannot pull ourselves up by our own bootlaces. We build bridges of prayer and service and repentance and these make us receptive to the forgiveness God is always offering to us. It does not *make* him forgive us as if he would not do so otherwise.

PRAYER TIME

This could be based around the 'Jesus Prayer': 'Lord Jesus Christ, son of the Living God, have mercy on me a sinner.'

17. What happens when I die?

AIM

The aim of this session is to impart the Christian understanding of resurrection and what it means for us.

ABOUT OURSELVES

Ask people to reflect for a moment on what they think death is. (You may do this by handing out a piece of paper on which is written at the top 'Death is . . .' and asking them to fill it in.)

INPUT

This might include:

(a) There is more than one kind of death (loss of a job, burglary, loss of a limb, etc. are all 'little deaths').

(b) Grief is a natural and normal part of our lives. As Christians we are not expected to stop grieving just because we believe life does not end in death.

(c) The resurrection of Jesus speaks to us of his power to conquer death – a power which is ours too. 'Because he died we shall live.'

(d) We do not know *exactly* what will happen when we die. We live by faith.

(e) The life of fullness Jesus promised is ours *now* but when we die we can live in closer union with God than before. This is not forced on us. If we want we can choose to reject God. Life without God is *hell*. Life with him in all his fullness is *heaven*. (This is true for the present as well as for the future.)

(f) Catholics believe that there will be a period after death of purification (or purgatory). This is *not* about sulphur and flames. It is a belief that having seen God face to face we shall *want* him to make us more like him before we enjoy the fullness of his presence for all eternity.

GROUP WORK

Read John 20:11–18.

How was Mary before she met the risen Christ?
How was Mary after she met the risen Christ?
How did Jesus' resurrection affect her?
How does Jesus' resurrection affect us?

PRAYER TIME

Place a crucifix and a vase of flowers for all to see.

Read: 1 Corinthians 15:51–55
Sing: A suitable Easter hymn

Notes

1. Be aware of those in the group who may have been recently bereaved or for whom the death of someone they love may be close.
2. Be prepared for a number of questions about hell and purgatory.

18. Who is the Holy Spirit?

AIM

The aim of this session is to introduce people to the Church's understanding of the Holy Spirit, who is active in the life of the Church today.

ABOUT OURSELVES

Ask people to share in pairs one experience when they were unable to find the right words to say in a particular situation. One person should do this and the other should listen in silence without comment. Roles should then be reversed. This activity should not take too long and should be done briefly.

Ask people to do the same exercise again, this time sharing

stories of when they were asked to do something that they felt they could not achieve. How did they feel?

INPUT

One member of the team should read Romans 8:26.
After a short pause another should read 1 Corinthians 12:4–7.
After a further pause another should read 1 Corinthians 12:3.

The leader should draw out from these three readings the following points:

(a) The Holy Spirit who is the Spirit of Jesus lives within us and helps us to find the right words to say both in our prayer and in our dealings with other people.
(b) The Holy Spirit is active within us, giving us gifts that enable us to do what God wishes to be done in his world today.
(c) The Holy Spirit lives within us, enabling us to live a life of faith and to come into a closer relationship with the Father.
(d) In all these ways the Holy Spirit gives life.

(You may want to talk here about the Spirit of God as portrayed in the Old Testament as the Giver of Life, and the Spirit of God as portrayed in the New Testament, who is the Spirit of the Life of Jesus let loose in the world.)

GROUP WORK

Give people a copy of Acts 2:1–21.

(a) What were the disciples feeling before the coming of the Spirit?
(b) What difference did the coming of the Spirit make to them?
(c) What difference did the coming of the Spirit make to those around them? Share this in the whole group.

PRAYER TIME

Either use a Pentecost hymn as a prayer or sing 'Veni Creator Spiritus' (Taizé chant).

Notes

1. You may have to talk about the tongues of fire and rushing wind and explain that the Bible often uses specific types of language when trying to explain the inexplicable or to describe the indescribable.
2. Running throughout this session should be the awareness of the living presence of the Holy Spirit *now*.
3. This session should be followed by one to do with helping people discover how the Holy Spirit works within themselves.

Chapter 4

TRAVELLING WITH OTHERS

Karen and John had been engaged for nine months when they first came into contact with St Joseph's. John was a Catholic but had not been a regular churchgoer for some years. Karen had never had anything to do with the Church. They wanted to be married in church, not just for social reasons but because they both felt it was the right thing to do. Neither of them could really explain in words why they thought like this but they knew it was important to them. They had been rather surprised that the parish priest had wanted to see them for more than just the usual fixing of dates and sorting out of arrangements. He had also introduced them to a married couple in the church family and suggested Karen and John should go along to the marriage preparation sessions the parish organized. Somewhat reluctantly they had done so and, to their surprise, had found them very helpful. 'It raised a lot of questions for us', said John. 'We began to see that there was more to Christianity than met the eye.'

As a result of that initial contact Karen and John had continued to have links, though not very strong ones, with St Joseph's after they were married. 'It was about a year later, when I discovered I was pregnant that we really got involved', explained Karen. 'We wanted to give the baby our best and we knew that must include some sort of religious upbringing but neither of us knew much about the Church or what it taught or what to do. I found it difficult to see why we needed to belong to a church at all. After all we could be good Christians on our own and John thought it all a bit irrelevant.'

Despite their misgivings John and Karen decided they should at least find out whether their local church had anything to offer. 'After all,' said John, 'we had been married there and we had a responsibility to our baby to explore what the church was all about.'

'We certainly gave them a hard time', grinned Karen. 'When I think of the statements we made and the questions we asked it was a wonder they didn't throw us out! We wanted honest answers about what the church was for, why it seemed so autocratic and why Catholic Christians seemed to us to go overboard on statues and saints and Mary.'

This chapter deals with questions about the church, what it is, what it is for and what place lay people have within it. It covers the topics of:

What is the Church?
What is the Church today?
How does the Church work?
Whose Church is it anyway? (2 sessions)
What do we have to share?
What is the difference? (2 sessions)

1. What is the Church?

AIM

The aim of this session is to give a basic understanding of what we mean by the Church and to encourage people to see the Church as the whole people of God.

ABOUT OURSELVES

Either in small groups or in the whole group, encourage people to share what the Church means for them. From this it should be possible to draw out a number of phrases, e.g. 'the family of God', 'the community that cares', etc.

INPUT

This should include the following concepts:

(a) *Ecclēsia* is the Greek word for 'church', meaning 'that which is called out'. God calls out his people. We become a church in so far as we respond to God's invitation to celebrate his presence, to listen to his word and to share his life.

(b) *Magisterium* usually refers to the teaching body of the Church, especially the bishops, led by the Pope, in succession from the Apostles and Peter.

(c) *Sensus fidelium* means 'understanding of the faithful'. The whole Church is the message of Christ, and the Holy Spirit's presence gives us the competence to keep this message and preach the gospel. So the whole of the Church cannot err in matters of faith.

DISCUSSION POINTS

(a) In what way are we called out by God and what are we called out for?

(b) St Paul calls the Church 'the body of Christ'. In our own body each part has its own functions. As members of the body of Christ, what gifts or functions do we use and what functions or talents might we develop?

(c) If we are the Church, what should we be doing for the community? Many people outside the Church think that membership is only for those who can keep the rules. Is that what we believe? To what degree do we accept those who break the rules?

PRAYER TIME

Read 1 Corinthians 12. Encourage people to think for a moment of their place in the Body of Christ and to thank God for it.

Close by saying together the 'Glory be to the Father . . .' If people are not familiar with this make sure they have a copy so they can join in.

2. What is the Church today?

AIM

To introduce people to some images or models of the Church and to help them explore what this means to them today.

OUR IMAGES

1. Work in pairs or small groups. Give each an envelope containing eight small pieces of paper on which are drawn:

   two people shaking hands
   a cross
   some money
   a family
   a bible
   a church building
   a sick person and visitor
   one blank piece for people to add their own drawing

These drawings need not be elaborate! Simple stick people will do as long as it is clear what each represents.

2. Ask people to arrange and stick their pictures on a large sheet of paper in whatever way they think best represents the Church. You may like to provide them with pens to make 'link lines' between the pictures if they wish. Encourage them to build up their own picture of the Church. Put these up for all to see and ask for clarification and/or explanation of what people want to convey.

INPUT

This might contain:

1. The idea that the Church pictures herself in different ways, as have the groups. These images are *complementary* to each other (as are the groups' pictures), not in competition. They add to the richness of the pattern which is the Church.
2. Some indication of how the Church understands herself in the following images:

(a)   The people of God.
(b)   The institutional Church.
(c)   The Body of Christ.
(d)   The servant Church.
(e)   The proclaiming Church.
(f)   The Church as sacrament. (See note 3 at the end of this session.)

3. Show how each image says something about God's relationship with his people and what the Church is for.

DISCUSS

What image of the local church do we have (do we see it primarily as an institution, a family, etc.?) and why?

What image of the Church does our local church convey to others? Would we want to convey anything else?

PRAYER TIME

Sing 'The Church's one foundation' or another suitable hymn on the theme of 'Church'.

Share together the sign of peace.

Notes

1. There is a great deal in this session and you may wish to divide it into two rather than rush it.
2. It is important to draw out how the pictures of the Church produced by the different groups *add* to the richness of the Church.
3. More information about images of Church and models of Church can be found in *Models of the Church* by Avery Dulles SJ (Gill & Macmillan).

3. How does the Church work?

AIM

The aim of this session is to give people an understanding of how the Church makes decisions and exercises authority. Begin the session with some basic input. This should include:

(a) The way the Church in its early history had to come to terms with new situations and especially with the move to accept Gentiles and to combat heresies. It might be a good idea just to outline the major heresies without going into so much detail that people get bogged down. At the risk of over-simplification, they are:

   Arius – who said that Jesus was not truly God.
   Nestorius – who said that Jesus had two persons, a human and a divine.
   Docetism – which stated that Jesus only seemed to be human but was really God.

These matters were dealt with by a series of Councils. Some of the statements of these Councils were in the form of Creeds.

(b) The way authority is exercised in the Church is through the hierarchy. Explain the roles of bishop, diocese, synods, councils, the Pope (you may need to stress here that not everything the Pope says on every subject is infallible!). At this point people who hold positions of responsibility within the Church could be invited to describe their role (make sure this is done *briefly*).

Alternatively, discuss:

(a) What specific instructions did Jesus give to his Apostles?
(b) How are these instructions carried out now?

(c)   What part do we have to play?

Allow time to gather responses together and for questions to be asked.

PRAYER TIME

Say together The Apostles' Creed (make sure people can see a copy).

Close with a suitable prayer.

Notes

1. Note the fairly lengthy *Input* for this session. A good deal of factual information is given here.
2. Try, where possible, when talking about the various difficulties the early Church had to face, to link them up with what is happening today (e.g. the idea that Jesus was not truly God or that he only seemed to be human are heresies that can still be found today).

For a fuller version of this material see Debbie Jones, *Focus on Faith*, Kevin Mayhew.

4. Whose Church is it anyway? (1)

AIM

To help participants explore the role of the laity in the Church today, in particular making the presence of Christ known in the secular world.

ABOUT GOD

1. Ask people to reflect on and then discuss what they think is God's purpose for his world. What is his design, his desire for the world he has created and what sort of world should it be?

   If you have done this in small groups gather these responses together.
2. Discuss together how God can bring his design to fruition.

INPUT

God can only carry out the design he has for the world through his people who live within it. The laity are called to:

(a) holiness;
(b) active membership of the Church;
(c) co-operation with God in building up the Kingdom of God within their own situations (you may need to explain the concept of the Kingdom more fully).

DISCUSSION

Discuss what it means in practice to build the Kingdom in the local situation. List three practical things.

ALTERNATIVE GROUP WORK

Read Matthew 13:31-32.

Using the image of the mustard tree, what 'branches' do you have in your community which shelter those who come?

How could you encourage new growth?

PRAYER TIME

Have a poster or slide of a secular situation in which God's love is shown (e.g. someone caring for others).

Read John 15:4-8.

Prayer:

Father, you call us to come to you and to be one with you. May we grow in holiness that others may see you in us. As branches of the vine may our lives reflect your presence and your kingdom come through us. We ask this through Jesus Christ our Lord.

Notes

1. It is important in this session to make sure that the discussion does not revolve around 'churchy' things, i.e. activities which take place *only* within the Christian community.
2. A good deal about the role of the laity in the secular world and the call to holiness can be found in *Christifideles Laici*, Apostolic Exhortation of Pope John Paul II.
3. You may need to explain carefully the concept of 'kingdom' and what the Church teaches regarding the building of the Kingdom and the laity's role in this task.

5. Whose Church is it anyway? (2)

AIM

The aim of this session is to explore the role of the laity in the active life of their local church.

ABOUT OUR CHURCH

Ask people to discuss the different events, groups and activities which happen in their church. You might like to ask people to do this before the session so that they can find out the answers to the following questions:

What happens in our church?
Who is involved?
Who is not involved?

You may need to make a list of these. It often surprises people just how much does go on.

INPUT

One member of the team should read 1 Corinthians 12:4–13. Correlation should now be drawn between the list of tasks mentioned by St Paul and those which take place in the local church community.

Emphasize:

(a) The Church is made up of people – all sorts and conditions with all sorts of gifts.
(b) We are all called to share in the life of the Church in some way.
(c) The Church is one unit or body. If *any* one part is missing, the body is not complete and does not operate properly.
(d) Everyone has some gift which can be used – we need a variety of gifts. The Church needs 'quiet gifts' as much as public ones.

Allow time for general discussion about this.

FOR REFLECTION

What is *my role* in the Church?

PRAYER TIME

Have a lighted candle on a table. Make sure there are no other visual distractions. Suggest that people write down on a small piece of paper what they think their own gift or role is in the Church. After a suitable hymn or prayer invite people to come and leave their papers around the candle as a sign of their commitment.

Notes

People may need help in 'translating' Paul's list of gifts in 1 Corinthians 12 to their own situation (e.g. healing includes doctors, nurses and counsellors, etc.).

6. What do we have to share?

AIM

The aim of this session is to help people discover and appreciate the gifts God has given them.

ABOUT OURSELVES

Ask people to reflect for a moment on someone they admire. What is it about that person that they appreciate? (If they wish they can share this in pairs or threes.)

INPUT

This should include:

(a) The concept that God holds every single person to be of infinite value and worth.
(b) God gives to each person some special gift, often unrecognized by us.
(c) These gifts are not optional extras – without them the Church is impoverished. God *needs* the gifts he has given to be used in order that his love can be shared.

GROUP WORK

If the group know each other quite well:

Seat the group in a circle. Hand each person a blank piece of paper and ask them to write their name at the top. Right at the bottom of the paper they should write what they think their gift is. They should then fold the paper up so that it cannot be seen. Pass the paper to the right. The next person should look at the name and write down what gift they think that person has. They should not look at what the person has written. The paper should be folded over and handed on. (No peeping is allowed!) When the papers have gone round the circle ask each person to open them and look at what other people said about them.

If the group do not know each other well:

Sitting in a circle, discuss what gifts lie amongst you.

PRAYER TIME

Use the parable of the talents (Matthew 25:14–30). Spend a moment reflecting on the gifts that you have and how you will use them.

Close with a suitable prayer.

Notes

1. Encourage people to speak about their gifts. Explain the difference between pride and acknowledging what has been given to you. No false modesty is allowed here. It is right that we should acknowledge our gifts.
2. If you are using the second form of group work, i.e. in a group where the members do not know each other well, make sure that the sharing of the gifts that lie amongst the group is done randomly and not in 'round the circle method'. This allows people to chip in and does not put them under pressure.
3. If you are using the first form of group work and have more than ten people you will need to form several circles.
4. The parable of the talents, used in the *Prayer time*, closes with condemnation of the one who fails to use the talent which has been given. You may need to talk about the strongly worded denunciation by Jesus of those who waste the gifts God has given and what this means.

(Group work exercise adapted from Anne Bishop and Eldon Hay, *Telling My Story, Sharing My Faith*, United Church of Canada.)

7. What's the difference? (1)

AIM

The aim of this session is to explore some 'Catholic specialities' and to explain their place in the life of the Catholic Christian.

This entire session could be carried out in the church building. It is important that people should *see* various items as they are explained to them, especially:

The Confessional or Reconciliation Room
Statues Include here explanations about the use of statues (that Catholics do not pray to statues but that they are visual aids).
Devotional articles such as the Rosary, candles, etc. Include here explanations about the Hail Mary and Sign of the Cross, the 'Glory Be', etc.

Allow plenty of time for questions (there are usually lots!).

Close with prayer, possibly the Hail Mary.

8. What's the difference? (2)

AIM

The aim of this session is to explore some areas of teaching which are specifically Catholic, especially what the Church teaches about Mary and the saints.

ABOUT OURSELVES

One member of the team should tell a story from his or her own experience about someone they have met whom they would call 'holy'.

(a) Who are the holy people you have met? What has been different about them? Share in pairs, threes or in a small group.

(b) What makes a saint? Have this discussion within the whole group.

INPUT

Include:

(a) Catholics do not pray to statues; they are visual aids. Catholics pray to God.

(b)   Catholics ask the saints to pray for them as they would ask any friend to do.

(c)   Mary is the greatest of these intercessors. The Church teaches that she is not only the Mother of Jesus but our Mother too. We ask her to intercede or pray for us. Catholics do not worship Mary. She is a creation of God as we are. Explain the Hail Mary if necessary.

PRAYER TIME

Sing: 'For all the Saints' or a suitable Marian hymn.

Father, we rejoice
that you have called women and men
throughout the ages into the family of your Church.
May we be filled with the Spirit that blessed their lives
and follow the example of your saints.

Chapter 5

STRENGTH FOR OUR TRAVELLING

Mandy had always been a Catholic, at least in name if not in practice. When she moved to a new home miles from the rest of her family she had felt lost and lonely at first but had soon found new friends and settled down. When she met Danny it was the proverbial love at first sight. They had married nine years ago and now had three children; the twins, Tony and Karen, were seven and Tom was four. The older children were at the Catholic school. First Communion was to take place in June. Mandy and Danny had been asked to attend special meetings for parents which would take place at the same time as the children were being prepared. Though they did not like to admit it, they found these meetings more useful than anything else at explaining what the Church taught about the Sacraments and why they were important in the world of today. So, when they heard that there was another chance to ask questions and find out more, they decided to take part in the parish 'Journey in Faith' meetings. Even though they were both Catholics already they were welcomed warmly for, as they were told, 'We all go on learning from one another about how God makes himself present to us and amongst us wherever we are on our journey in life'.

These sessions deal with how God gives us strength on our journey. They include the concept of sacrament and what this means in the life of the individual Christian. There is also material on specific sacraments, as well as sessions that consider other ways in which our relationship with God is strengthened and developed.

Sessions in this chapter cover:

What is a sacrament?
What is Baptism?
What is Confirmation?
What is the Eucharist?
What is Reconciliation?
What is Anointing of the Sick?
What is Marriage?

What is Holy Orders?
What is the Liturgy for?
How can I pray with others?

1. What is a sacrament?

AIM

The aim of this session is to explore what the word 'sacrament' means.

ABOUT OURSELVES

Ask people to give examples of some of the symbols used in everyday life (e.g. flags, flowers, etc.). Explore together what these symbols are saying.

INPUT

This might include:

(a)   Examples of how we use things and words in a symbolic way, e.g. flowers to say 'welcome' or a kiss to express affection.

(b)   The difference between a symbol and a sacrament.

(c)   Jesus as the sacrament of God, i.e. the way God is made present to us.

(d)   The Church as the sacrament of Jesus, i.e. Jesus' life and work is found in its clearest form in the Church.

(e)   The sacraments of the Church (the way in which the Church expresses the presence of Jesus who lives within it).

(f)   A sacrament as an 'outward sign of inward grace'.

FOR DISCUSSION

What actions, things or words have a special importance for you? (Share this in pairs.)

In what way do you experience a real sense of God's presence, through a symbolic action or event or thing?

What does it mean to say that Jesus is the sacrament of God's presence for us today?

PRAYER TIME

Have available a wide range of symbols, e.g. pictures, poems, flowers, candles, crucifixes, rosaries, etc. Allow people to choose one and to reflect upon it quietly on their own. Some quiet music might be useful for this exercise. Encourage people to think about what the symbol tells them about God and their relationship with him.

Notes

1. It is important to be clear about the distinction between signs, symbols and sacrament.
2. It is important to explain that, whereas we often use the words 'symbol' or 'sign' as meaning something that is not quite real (e.g. 'This is only a sign of what I meant' or 'This is only a symbol of my respect'), the Church does the opposite. Symbols express the deepest reality.
3. Symbol and sacrament have an ability to reach deep within us in a way that words cannot.

2. What is Baptism?

AIM

The aim of this session is to explore the various fundamental elements of Baptism and to show its importance.

ABOUT OURSELVES

Ask people to share a recollection of a baptism. What stood out for them?

Brainstorm these onto a flip-chart or overhead projector.

What questions do these recollections raise? (The leader should go through the responses highlighting the questions – at this stage the aim is to discover the questions, not to give the answers.)

INPUT

Have the various symbols which are used at a celebration of Baptism present for all to see.

Either

1. Use these symbols to talk about the rite and what it means

or

2. Explain the themes associated with Baptism as the basis for the input. This should include:

(a) Baptism brings us into a special relationship with God.
(b) Baptism makes us members of the Church.
(c) Baptism starts us on a journey of new life (we die with Christ and we rise to new life with him).
(d) Baptism is about a turning away from self-centredness (original sin). We do this by making three promises to reject all that is evil.
(e) Baptism allows us (or our parents and god-parents on our behalf) to profess our faith. We do this by answering three questions.

GROUP WORK

Richard and Mary have two children. The first was baptized but there has never been any real link with the church since the day of the Baptism. They have come requesting Baptism for their second child.

What should be the response of the Christian community to Richard and Mary? Should Baptism:

(a) be administered regardless of the faith of the parents and, if so, why?
(b) be delayed and, if so, why?

Allow time for general discussion.

PRAYER TIME

Place the symbols of Baptism in a focal position. Make sure you have a paschal candle (and explain its meaning if you have not already done so at some other time during the session).

Give to each person a small candle.

Let each person light their candle from the paschal candle as a sign of their commitment to follow the way of Christ, to reject evil and to walk in the newness of life.

A suitable hymn could be sung or quiet music played during this time.

Notes

1. Allow time for questions after the *Input*. It is important to clear up misunderstandings about what happens to people who are *not* baptized. Expect questions about limbo, hell and original sin.
2. If necessary go through the Rite in more detail. This may well entail another session but it is important to do this if people are to be baptized at the Easter Vigil. They should be clear about what is expected of them, what the Church proclaims about their new beginning in Christ, and what the symbols really mean.

3. What is Confirmation?

AIM

The aim of this session is to explore the meaning of the sacrament of Confirmation and its relevance for our journey of faith.

ABOUT OURSELVES

Share in pairs or small groups one skill you know you have.

What is the skill?
How did you discover it?
How was it developed?
Who helped you to develop it?

(There is no need to report the findings of this discussion.)

INPUT

Explain:

Confirmation is a sacrament of initiation (together with Baptism and the Eucharist). It is difficult to see it apart from these two sacraments. In the early days, and in some parts of the Church today, all three sacraments are administered together on one occasion, children included. We do this for adults.

Confirmation *confirms our Baptism*. We are drawn more deeply into the relationship God has established with us.

Confirmation *celebrates the power and the work of the Holy Spirit* among us and in us. It is about the gifts given to us (Galatians 5:22–23; 1 Corinthians 12:4–13).

Confirmation gives us the power of the Holy Spirit *to be the body of Christ* in the world today.

Explain the gestures and symbols used in Confirmation.

GROUP WORK

If you had the opportunity to write the bidding prayers for the Confirmation, what would you pray for?

PRAYER TIME

Use the prayers people have composed.

Notes

1. You may have to edit the prayers for use in the closing prayer if you have too many.
2. Stress that Confirmation is *not* primarily a sacrament of commitment although there is obviously that element within it. It is a sacrament of initiation and properly belongs with Baptism.
3. The history of how the sacrament has developed explains a good deal about the confusion that sometimes surrounds it. An excellent explanation of how we have arrived at our present situation can be found in William Bausch, *A New Look at the Sacraments* (XXIII Publications).

(This section is adapted from Nigel Bavidge, *The Sacrament Explained,* Kevin Mayhew.)

4. What is the Eucharist?

AIM

The aim of this session is to enable people to grasp the centrality of the Eucharist in the life of the Church.

ABOUT OURSELVES

Ask people to imagine the fire brigade has requested them to leave their home due to the danger of a nearby fire. They are allowed to take only a few articles with them. They must choose *one* article given to them as a present by someone else to take with them.

What gift would they take?
Why do they treasure it so much?

Share with each other.

INPUT

This should include:

(a) When a person gives us a gift they express their love for us. Jesus is God's gift to us. He is the gift of God's love.

(b) His death shows us the depth of God's love. His life and his death were a sacrifice of love.

(c) The Eucharist makes Jesus' sacrifice of love present for us.

(d) At the Last Supper Jesus gave himself to his friends in the form of bread and wine so that they could be always united with him. He does the same for us.

(e) At the Last Supper Jesus took, gave thanks, broke and shared bread and wine. These four elements can be seen in the Eucharist.

(f) In the bread and wine Christ is present. It becomes his Body and Blood.

The significance of bread:

Bread is a staple food. It is life-giving. The Eucharist also is life-giving. We need to be sustained by the Body and Blood of Jesus if we are to live his life.

God fed the people with manna in the wilderness to give them strength. We need to be nourished by God as we travel on our journey of faith.

Bread has a particular importance for the poor because they need it to live. Without the presence of God we miss out on life-giving food.

Bread must be broken if it is to be shared. We see how deep is God's love for us in the broken body of Jesus on the cross.

· Bread must be shared. The Eucharist is not simply a private act of devotion, it is a community meal. We share in Christ's life as members of a family.

The significance of wine:

Wine is a sign of healing. (The Good Samaritan poured wine and oil on the wounds of the injured traveller.) Wine is life-giving. The Eucharist is life-giving and healing.

Wine is a sign of joy. We rejoice in the depths of God's love for us and his presence with us.

Wine is a sign of blessing. God rejoices in us.

Wine is for sharing. We have entered into a relationship with God which we share with others.

GROUP WORK

Give everyone the following story to discuss.

> A few years ago, at Mass one morning, the priest broke the bread. In the quiet of the church the sound of the host being broken resounded. It suddenly struck me that every time I go to Communion I ask to become like Jesus and that means to be taken, broken and given away.
>
> That morning I knew that, even though I had been given something very real every time I had been to Communion, I had never yet truly accepted all that is means. Perhaps that is what true holiness is – being prepared to be taken, broken and given away. I hope that, every time I go to Communion, I come one step nearer to accepting that invitation.

What does this say to you? What could it mean for your life?

PRAYER TIME

Have a chalice, grapes, a bottle of wine and a loaf of bread displayed on a table.

Have a moment of quiet reflection.

Read: Matthew 26:26–29.
Sing: 'This is my body, broken for you' (Damian Lundy).

or

'Lord Jesus Christ you have come to us' (Patrick Appleford).

Notes

1. You may wish to use more than one session to explore this theme. There is obviously a great deal more that could be said in relation to the Eucharist (e.g. Passover, various names given to the celebration, etc.).
2. Explain carefully the meaning of 'Do this in memory'. This means to make present now – not merely to bring to mind.
3. There is no need to gather together the results of the final discussion. Make sure, however, that you leave time for questions.

(Adapted from Nigel Bavidge, *The Sacraments Explained*, Kevin Mayhew.)

5. What is Reconciliation?

AIM

The aim of this session is to explore what the sacrament of Reconciliation means in the life of the Christian today.

Invite questions about this sacrament from the group. If you like, you can ask people in smaller groups to decide on one question they wish to ask. Make a list of these which can be clearly seen.

Ask people to complete the sentence 'Sin is . . .' Again list these.

INPUT 1

Use the three names for this sacrament as the basis for explaining the purpose of the sacrament.

First, refer to sin as

(a) the breaking of a relationship (not just rules);
(b) a symptom of our desire to go our own way;
(c) a dis-ease which needs healing.

Secondly, refer to the name most commonly used for celebrating this sacrament:

Confession – This tells us the sacrament is about admitting that we have broken our relationship with God and with other people and how we have done so.

Thirdly, refer to the second name given to this sacrament:

Reconciliation – This tells us that the purpose of the sacrament is to reunite us with God and each other. We are to be reconciled and, in being reconciled, we are healed.

Penance – This has nothing to do with making God forgive us. It is an expression of our sorrow and our willingness to do better. (Explain what form this penance usually takes.)

Finally, stress that the sacrament should be a joyful celebration of God's love. We need to prepare well for it, celebrate it and thank God for the new life we have.

GROUP WORK

Which of these three names do you like best and why?

INPUT 2

Explain carefully exactly how the sacrament is celebrated. Go through the Rite (A) and allay any fears people may have. Explain the role of the priest in the sacrament. Allow time for questions.

PRAYER TIME

Allow time for people to think about their own relationship with God. (If you wish you could use a short examination of conscience but, if so, choose it carefully or write one yourself.)
   Say together 'I confess . . .' from the Order of Mass.

Notes

1. If you have not already done so, show people the confessional or reconciliation rooms.
2. If possible, one or more of the team members should talk about their own experience of what the sacrament means to them.
3. Make sure you have covered the questions people listed at the start of the session.
4. Make sure you have cleared up any misconceptions (e.g. Confession means you can confess the sin on Saturday and do it again on Sunday!).

6. What is Anointing?

AIM

The aim of this session is to introduce people to the sacrament of Anointing the Sick and to show its purpose.

STORY

One member of the team should read the following story or one like it.

> Peter had just come home from hospital. He was still quite weak from an operation to remove a tumour from his lung. As far as he knew the operation had been a complete success. He would have to go back for further treatment but the surgeon had said they had

removed the diseased lung and there were no secondary growths. Yet Peter did not feel at ease. He was still worried. The fact that cancer had been found in his body at all made him feel somehow unclean. He knew with his mind that it was quite an irrational way to think but he could not help it. He was depressed and anxious despite all the good news. His body was mending well but the rest of him had not yet come to terms with what had happened.

BRAINSTORM

Sickness affects the whole of us – not just our bodies. What help would benefit Peter the most?

Break into small units and give each group one of the following passages to read:

Luke 13:10–17
Luke 18:35–43
Mark 7:31–37
Mark 2:1–12
Mark 1:40–45

What is Jesus' attitude to sick people?
What does he actually do to heal them?

Share your findings.

INPUT

Draw out from the gospel stories:

(a) Jesus realizes sickness is not the will of God. (Be clear about the difference between God allowing sickness and God willing it.) Jesus wishes people to be released from the power of sickness.

(b) Jesus' attitude is one of compassion and understanding.

(c) Jesus realizes that physical sickness is only one side of the coin. When we are physically ill we are affected mentally and spiritually (hence Jesus' reference to sin being forgiven when he heals the sick of the palsy). Jesus heals the whole person, not just the body.

(d) Jesus realizes the importance of touch in healing.

(e) Jesus realizes the importance of the community. Hence his command to the leper to go back to the community and become reinstated within it.

(f) The sacrament of Anointing has all these elements within it.

The Church continues to do what Jesus did.

i It gives strength to release people from the power of dis-
ease.

ii It is for the healing of the whole person.

iii Physical touch is part of this sacrament.

iv It is celebrated by the Church, i.e. it is the 'elders of the
church' (James 5:14–16), the leaders of the community,
who lay hands on the sick person.

v Oil is used because it was, and still is, used in the preparation of ointment. It heals and soothes. Athletes use oil
in preparation for activity. The oil used in anointing
reminds us of the strength God gives. Oil is used as a sign
of a setting apart to do God's work. Monarchs, priests and
prophets were anointed for this reason. We are invited to
consecrate and use our sickness as part of God's work.

IN GROUPS

Does it make any sense to say that our pain can be used as
part of God's saving work? Think of an example.

PRAYER TIME

Say together Psalm 23.

Pray for those you know who are sick that they may have
healing, strength and peace.

Notes

1. Make sure people are clear about the place of disease in Christian
thinking. We do not have a clear-cut answer to the problem of
pain but we do have some clues about it.

2. If you have time, or during another session if necessary, go
through the Rite of Anointing, exploring the different parts of the
Rite and how it links up with our understanding of a God of
healing and love.

3. Be very sensitive to any in the group who may have recently
suffered, or watched someone else suffer.

4. Be clear that this sacrament is not only for physical illness and
not only for the dying.

7. What is Marriage?

AIM

The aim of this session is to help people explore the Christian understanding of marriage in the world of today.

Share in pairs one incident in your life when you have been conscious of God calling you to do something or to change. This need not be anything spectacular – an example of a 'guilty conscience' leading to change is enough. (If possible, one member of the team should give an example from his or her own life to get people started.)

INPUT

This might include:

1. Marriage is a vocation. Some people are called to remain single, some to serve God in a particular way as priests or religious, some are called to marriage. No one calling is 'superior' to the others. They are different and God calls different people to different life-styles. Each has something to offer to 'building up the Body of Christ', the Church, and each has a witness to the love of God which is unique.

2. Marriage is a gift of one person to another. It reflects God's gift of himself to each one of us. His gift was total. In marriage two people give themselves to each other for life. So marriage reflects something of God's relationship with all his people. (In the Scriptures this relationship is often spoken of in marriage terms.)

3. Marriage is about support and growth. In their life together the couple are called to co-operate with God in helping each other grow into God's likeness.

4. Marriage is about other people. Although the couple are called to love each other exclusively in this special way, this does not mean they are to stop loving others. Marriage is to be a sort of visual aid to show what loving is about. The couple are to help each other grow in love but also to be the first teachers of their children in the ways of love and to be outgoing in love for others. A married couple is the Church in miniature.

5. Marriage is about mission. When we are baptized we share

the work of Christ. The couple work for the good of each other, their family and those whose lives they touch.

GROUP WORK

Give out the following:

Modern society has made many people look again at what marriage is all about. The expectations people have are different:

- The role of women has changed radically. No longer are they seen as dependent on men but as equals. (Not everyone is convinced: there's a lot more work to do!)
- Women, therefore, have new expectations of life. They want to find new ways of fulfilling themselves as people. Being a wife and mother (roles which gave women meaning and purpose only in relation to other people) is, for many, not enough.
- Employment patterns have changed. Many families need both parents to work to support the life-style they want.
- Because many people have to move away from home to find employment, the extended family network, which was a great source of support for married couples, has to a great extent broken down.
- Because of developments in medical science, couples can choose to limit family size and decide much more easily when to have children.
- Improved medical care and treatment mean that people live longer and, therefore, marriages last longer.
- There has been a growing understanding among married people that sex is about much more than having children.
- Divorce is now acceptable in society and quiet easily available.

How do you think these issues have affected people's expectations of marriage?

Are there others you would add?

(Adapted from Nigel Bavidge, *The Sacraments Explained*, Kevin Mayhew.)

Conclude with a reflection on what the Christian understanding of Marriage has to say about these issues. (Make sure this is positive and not negative.)

PRAYER TIME

Sing: 'Lead us, heavenly Father, lead us'.

Pray that we may live our lives aware of God's calling to share his love.

Pray for all married couples.

Notes

1. Be very careful in this session not to give the impression that marriage is the only way of life if people are not priests or religious. Be sensitive to the single people present.
2. Be conscious of those in difficult or broken marriage relationships.
3. Do not idealize marriage beyond recognition!
4. Be aware that people may have questions about the Church's teaching regarding mixed marriages, annulment and divorce.

8. What is Holy Orders?

AIM

The aim of this session is to help people understand the role of the priest in the Church today and the calling we all have to share in Christ's priesthood.

STORY

Debbie had never thought much about God. That was until she met Jan. Jan was a busy mother of four teenagers who also worked as a nurse *and* seemed to have abundant energy for dozens of other activities as well. The Richardson household was always 'open house' with people dropping in for a chat and a kettle that seemed permanently on the boil. Debbie suspected that half the time the family never knew who was in what room. Yet despite the hustle and bustle, Jan was the sort of person who seemed to exist in a pool of peace and, if anyone needed to sit and talk, then Jan gave the impression that everything else, no matter how urgent, could wait. Her whole attention was on what was being said. She seemed to have that marvellous gift of living every moment to the full. Debbie's awareness of God came through Jan. There was a sense in which she saw the love, concern and patience of God in the love, concern and patience of Jan.

REFLECT

Ask people to reflect for a moment on one incident in their lives where they experienced God through the life of another person. (One member of the team should share such a story.)

INPUT

This should include:

1. We are all called to minister God to each other. At our Baptism we entered into a special relationship with God. We share in the priesthood of Christ.
2. God calls different people to undertake different tasks. In this way his love is shared among us.
3. In the Church we all have a part to play. Some are called to the specific function of priesthood. The Church talks about the priesthood of the faithful (the sharing in Christ's work we all have by virtue of our Baptism) and the ministerial priesthood (the calling of some to serve God as the leaders of the local Christian community).
4. Those who serve God in this way do so when they are ordained (The Sacrament of Holy Orders). Ordination is restricted to men, who must be and remain single. (Celibacy is required in the western Church.)
5. A priest is one who:

i Presides for the community. He is the focus of the family gathered together for the Eucharist, at which he speaks the words of Christ. He leads the community in celebrating God's presence.

ii Cares for the community. He is the leader who leads by serving others.

iii Represents the wider Church for the community. The priest is the representative of the bishop.

iv Serves not only the local church community but is responsible (sent) to the wider community as well.

v Speaks the words of God to the community. He thus proclaims God's message of love, pardon for sin and assurance of forgiveness. His task is to encourage and guide.

vi Teaches in order that members of the community may understand their faith and share God's love with other people.

vii Acts in the name of Christ. Today priests share much of their work with the laity, whose activity is complementary to his. The Church needs both.

GROUP WORK

Read John 10 (give this out so that every person can have a copy).

What does this image used by Jesus of himself say to us about what it means to be a priest?

PRAYER TIME

Read Ephesians 4:1–13.

Pray that we may all respond to God's call to serve him.

Pray for the priests of the local and wider Church.

Notes

1. If a priest is present it would be helpful for him to talk from personal experience about what it means to be a priest today and, in particular, the way priest and lay person can work together.
2. Be prepared for questions about celibacy and women priests.
3. Explain carefully the place of authority in the Church today.
4. If necessary, explain the relationship between bishop, priest and deacon, how they differ and what they have in common but do not get too bogged down in this.

9. What is the Liturgy for?

AIM

The aim of this session is to introduce people to the concept of prayer and worship and to explore why liturgy is central to the life of the Church.

BRAINSTORM

List the different things that go on during a church service. Ask people to call these out, e.g. prayers, readings, hymns, offertory procession, etc.

List who takes part, e.g. readers, choir, Eucharistic ministers, priest, etc.

INPUT

This should include:

(a) The Eucharist is the Liturgy of the Church. It is the central point of our life.
(b) The Eucharistic Liturgy is divided into two main parts,

the Liturgy of the Word and the Liturgy of the Eucharist. We are fed through *both* of these; by the Word of God and the Bread of Life.

(c) Worship is about giving God his 'worth-ship'. It is the way we acknowledge his worthiness to be praised. This is the primary activity of the Church.

(d) Worship should be centred on God, not on ourselves.

(e) Worship is bringing our praise to God and receiving new life and strength from God.

(f) Worship is a communal activity, we do it together.

(g) We express that this is a communal act by the way different tasks are given to different people.

(h) Worship is concerned with the whole of us, not just our minds (hence the need for movement, colour, music, etc.).

(i) We worship out of love, not out of fear.

GROUP WORK

1. What do you like about the Liturgy? What do you dislike?
2. Do we go to church to put something in or to get something out?

PRAYER TIME

Use the Liturgy of the Word from the Order of Mass as the basis of this (i.e. from the beginning of Mass until the end of the Bidding Prayers). Choose appropriate readings and a closing prayer.

Notes

1. The *Prayer time* will probably take longer than usual for this session.
2. Allow time for some response from the group work about likes and dislikes and also about the question of how much we give and how much we receive through the Liturgy.
3. Stress throughout the *Input* that worship is an expression of our response to God's love for us.

10. How can I pray with others?

AIM

The aim of this session is to give people an experience of a non-eucharistic act of worship which they have created themselves.

Step 1

Explain the aim of this session. Stress:

(a) Worship of this type can be done by anyone. There does not need to be a priest present.
(b) Worship of this type needs to be structured.
(c) Worship is the focus of our life together as a Christian community. It acknowledges that God is at the centre of our life.
(d) We celebrate our faith together by using the gifts God has given us.

Step 2

Choose a theme. This is best done by the members of the group themselves. Sometimes a theme may be obvious because of the time of year or something which has happened in the group. If no obvious theme arises it may be necessary for leaders to suggest several and let people choose.

Step 3

Divide the group into the following sections. (It is best to allow people to choose the one they feel most suits them.) Encourage the faint-hearted if necessary!

Music (to choose hymns and songs related to the theme)

Art (to produce a focal point and suitable visual aids related to the theme, e.g. a poster, etc.)

Prayer (to write an opening and closing prayer and bidding prayers related to the theme)

Readings (to choose suitable Scripture readings and, if necessary, 'secular' readings related to the theme)

Drama (to produce a short dramatic interpretation of the theme)

Step 4

Allow the various groups to work with the theme. (They will need at least forty minutes.) Someone will need to act as 'go-between' in order to convey to the various groups what the others are doing.

It is easiest to shape the celebration according to the Liturgy of the Word at Mass, with drama instead of the homily. Secular readings and songs can be interposed within this basic structure.

Members of the various groups are responsible for presenting their 'parts', e.g. the prayer group does all the prayers, etc.

Write up the order of service for all to see and to avoid intrusive announcements.

Make sure the seating is suitable (avoid sitting in rows if possible) and make sure everyone can see the focal point.

Step 5
Celebrate the Act of Worship together.

Notes

1. Encourage people a good deal in this session. Confidence is often lacking but be positive and affirming so that people are willing to 'give it a go'. Show confidence in the group.
2. Do not be afraid that the worship will not come together! It always does and people are far more talented than we usually imagine.
3. Allow people to opt for the group in which they will feel most comfortable but do not allow people to opt out. If necessary, make sure one of the team is in each group to help inspire confidence.
4. Take your time over the celebration itself and, if possible, allow people to discuss it afterwards.

Chapter 6

TRAVELLING RESPONSIBLY

Rachel had only become involved in the life of the local church
because she had taken part in a sponsored swim to raise money
for a village in India. She was not what you would call a
particularly religious person, at least she did not think so, and
she certainly never went to church on Sunday. As far as she
could see it did not seem to have much relevance to her life
and certainly not to people who were less well off than her.

Rachel did, however, have a very highly developed sense of
justice. She would get really annoyed at anything she thought
was unfair or unjust. If the church had something to say about
putting the wrongs of the world right then it might have more
to commend it. She had seen precious little sign of it before
her friend, Sheila, asked her to take part in the fund-raising
swim. Rachel was soon involved with the justice and peace
group and found that there were other people like her who
felt responsible for the way the world was shaped and who
were trying, in however small a way, to build a better society.

So, Rachel became involved with the church but it was questions about what was right and what was wrong that attracted
her to it. She knew that there were no easy answers and she
would have distrusted any group which claimed to have *the*
answer for every single individual situation. What she did
appreciate was the fact that the church offered clear guidance
and ways of looking at issues which helped her to come to her
own decisions about what she could do.

This chapter looks at questions of justice, peace and morality,
both personal and corporate.

It covers:

How do I decide what is right?
Who is important?
How can I help to make a better world?
What about my relationships with others?
What does the Church say about sex?
Justice – whose responsibility?

1. How do I decide what is right?

AIM

The aim of this session is to help people explore the various factors involved in making a moral decision and to offer guidelines which will help them do so in the light of the Church's teaching.

ABOUT OURSELVES

In small groups or pairs or threes, discuss:

Suppose a friend of yours tells you that he or she is going to deliberately refuse to declare some income to the Inland Revenue. What motive would be most likely to alter his or her mind?

Would it be

(a)   fear of getting caught?
(b)   knowledge of breaking the law?
(c)   feeling guilty?
(d)   belief in the rights of others?

If you wish, you can have some feedback from this exercise but it is not integral to the session.

INPUT

This should include:

(a)   Awareness that a moral decision is usually made by the combination of a number of factors.
(b)   When we are making a moral decision we need to bear in mind four elements:

   i   We need to look at the gospel values – what does Scripture say in response to the moral question? (Love, faithfulness, hope, joy, peace, patience, kindness, gentleness, justice, goodness, truth, chastity, courage, etc.)

   ii   We need to consider the facts and findings of the world around us that have a bearing on the question.

   iii   We need to take into account our individual circumstances, the here-and-now situation in which we, the decision-makers, find ourselves. We need to consider our strengths and limitations.

iv We need to consider the tradition of the Church and her teachings. What does the wisdom of the Church have to say that bears on our question?

(c) We need to ask – will our response be life-serving, faithful to God, faithful to the Church?

(d) The teaching of the Church is usually of a general nature. It cannot possibly legislate for every single individual circumstance. So we each have a responsibility to follow our own conscience.

(e) Conscience is our primary guide but conscience needs to be formed in the light of what the Scriptures and Church have to say. We have not been left in the dark.

(f) In the end we are responsible for our own decisions.

GROUP WORK

Give every small group the following story:

James was feeling very pleased with himself. He had been saving hard to buy a small computer. He had struggled to do this by cutting down on some of the other things he wanted to buy. When he received an unexpected gift of £100 he was over the moon. Now he had enough to make his purchase and have some left over. On the very day he received the cheque, the evening news on the television was full of pictures of starving children in Africa. A nagging thought persisted in James' mind. Ought he really to buy the computer or should he give the £100 to save lives? On the one hand the money had been given to him and he could hardly turn around to his benefactor and say he had given it away. On the other he wondered if he could justify spending it on himself when people were dying. Perhaps he should give away the money he had left over. He told himself that a few more months would not matter and he could always tell the giver that he was intending to buy a computer soon. He also told himself that the computer would be very helpful for his work and would probably help him to earn more in the long run, which he could then give away. How to spend his money wisely and how to account for it in the light of his faith was a decision he would have to face many times.

If you were James what would you do and why?

PRAYER TIME

Using an overhead projector or a large poster display the words from Micah 6:8.

He has told you, O mortal, what is good;
and what does the Lord require of you
but to do justice, and to love kindness,
and to walk humbly with your God?

Ask people to meditate on the three phrases:

do justice
love kindness
walk humbly

Pray for:
Forgiveness for the times we have failed to act in those ways.
Courage to follow the three ways in the future.

Notes

1. It is important to be clear that the Church gives moral norms. It does not give a set of rules for every single individual circumstance. Make sure that people are clear about this. You may like to use the illustration of a road sign. It is there to prevent people getting hurt, but it is up to the individual driver as to the action he or she takes in the light of the sign.
2. It would be a good idea to accompany this session with some handouts giving guidelines on what the Church teaches about particular moral dilemmas (e.g. euthanasia, abortion, just war, capital punishment, contraception, etc.).

2. Who is important?

AIM

The aim of this session is to help participants realize that as Christians we are called to follow Jesus' example of caring for each individual and showing dignity to each person.

Begin by reading to the group Matthew 9:18–26. (This is best done by four people, one taking the part of Jesus, one that of the official, one the woman and one the narrator.)

While he was saying these things to them, suddenly a leader of the synagogue came in and knelt before him, saying, 'My daughter has just died; but come and lay your hand on her, and she will live.' And Jesus got up and followed him, with his disciples. Then suddenly a woman who had been suffering from hemorrhages for twelve years came up behind him and touched the fringe of his cloak, for she said to herself, 'If I only touch his cloak, I will be made well.' Jesus turned and seeing her he said, 'Take heart, daughter; your faith has made you well.' And instantly the woman was made well. When Jesus came to the leader's house and saw the flute players and the crowd making a commotion, he said, 'Go away; for the girl is not dead but sleeping.' And they laughed at him. But when the crowd had been put outside, he went in and took her by the hand, and the girl got up. And the report of this spread throughout that district.

Split into four groups.

Ask each group to take one role. One group should play the part of the official, one group take the role of the woman who was healed, one group take the role of Jesus and one group that of the crowd of mourners.

Ask each group to go through the story working out how they would react as the events unfold. Allow some time for this.

When the groups are ready come back into one unit (but the groups should remain together).

The leader should go through the story asking for comment from each of the groups as the story unfolds.

What were their reactions to each other as the event progresses?
How did they feel?
What did they want to do?

All comments should be directed through the leader, who should concentrate on drawing out the way Jesus reacted to each person and how they responded to him.

INPUT

This should include:

(a) Jesus' attitude is one which accepts people where they are.
(b) Jesus has time for people.
(c) Jesus responds to people no matter what their social status (i.e. the woman was unclean).
(d) Jesus wants the best for people.
(e) Jesus goes out of his way to help them.
(f) These characteristics of Jesus should be ours.

PRAYER TIME

Say together:

> God be in my head
> and in my understanding.
> God be in my eyes
> and in my looking.
> God be in my mouth
> and in my speaking.
> God be in my heart
> and in my thinking.
> God be at mine end
> and at my departing.
>
> (Sarum Primer, 1527)

Notes

1. Do not let the group get out of hand when they are immersing themselves in the story.
2. Make sure the *Input* helps to de-role people.
3. Draw out from people the importance in the story of Jesus' openness to the people who came to him and the importance of this for us.
4. If necessary make sure you deal with the question of Jesus' apparent impatience with the crowd.

3. How can I help to make a better world?

AIM

The aim of this session is to enable people to consider ways in which they can co-operate with God in his work of building the Kingdom.

ABOUT OURSELVES

Ask people to list the elements they think would go to make up a perfect world.

One member of the team should read the following story (copies should be available for everyone to have *after* the story has been read).

Maria belonged to St Martin's church. She lived about half a mile away and from her window she looked out at a home for elderly people. It was a beautiful new complex with all that the residents could wish for in the way of amenities. It had been opened a year before and the residents were now part of the street's community. Maria noticed, however, that very few of them went far from their own front door. One day she was having a leisurely chat with Arthur. 'The problem is', he said, 'the bus stop is in the wrong place. If they would only re-route it up and around this street instead of stopping it at the bottom of the hill we could all get out and about much more.' 'Why don't you see the powers that be?' asked Maria. 'Oh, believe me we've tried. We seem to get nowhere.'

Maria was now undecided about whether or not to do what her conscience told her to do. In the end she decided that she must do something, so, taking a day off work, she presented herself at the offices of the local bus company. She got no joy. Next she wrote – still nothing. A petition from the residents and other local people didn't seem to be doing much although Maria thought she noticed a slight weakening in the last letter she received: 'The matter would be reconsidered.' Months went by and Maria's enquiries were met by the all-too-familiar brick wall. Eventually she contacted the local paper and the local radio station, which featured what had now become a major local issue. It took Maria and a small group of people from her church eighteen months to get the bus re-routed but she and her supporters did it in the end. Now the residents have a fuller life, and they have access to the world outside their front door. It has not, however, made much difference to the number of those who come to church. 'Why did you do it?' asked Arthur one day. 'Because it was right to do it and because it would be hypocritical of us to sit in our church on Sunday and do nothing,' replied Maria.

(From Christine Dodd, *Called to Mission*, Geoffrey Chapman)

With the whole group, brainstorm.

1. Why do you think Maria's conscience was troubled when she first realized what was happening?
2. What qualities do you see in Maria that enabled her to act as she did?

INPUT

This should include:

1. Christians are called to be involved in the world God has

made. Our calling is *not* to be removed from the world but to transform it.

2. In order to co-operate with God in his action we need to challenge what is wrong.
3. In order to co-operate with God in his activity we need to support the good which is there.
4. In order to co-operate with God in building a better world we need to

(a) *look* at the world in which we live and not run away from it;
(b) *make decisions* about the world in which we live in the light of our faith and what we believe about God;
(c) *engage in activity* which will enable God's kingdom to come in all its fullness.

GROUP DISCUSSION

What stops us as individuals and the group from the task of building a better world?
(Give people large sheets of paper on which to record their answers.)

What, in practice, can we do to help build a better world?
(Responses to this should also be listed on large sheets of paper. Allow time for people to discover what each group has recorded.)

PRAYER TIME

Have a picture of a present-day situation in which the building of a better world needs to be accomplished.

Use an Act of Contrition, in which we express our sorrow for our failures to take responsibility, and a Prayer of Commitment to do more in the future.

Notes

1. There is a great temptation for people to make sweeping generalizations, especially in the *Group discussion* for this session. Try to ensure that people are making comments that are relevant to their own situations.
2. Aid societies such as CAFOD, Christian Aid, etc. produce many posters and pictures which can be used for the Liturgy and for other visual aids throughout this session.

3. Make sure you explain what an Act of Contrition is if you have not already done so.

4. What about my relationship with others?

AIM

The aim of this session is to help people explore the Christian understanding of respect for and responsibility towards the individual.

Begin this session with a short time of reflection. Have a time of quiet prayer asking people to focus on the person or persons they care about most.

In pairs share together what it is about the person that most endears him or her to you. Ask people to call out *in general terms* the qualities that they have discussed.

INPUT

This should include:

1. An outline of the list of qualities given by St Paul when he speaks about the Christian's relationship to others (Galatians 5:22).
   Christians are to be:

   loving
   joyful
   full of peace
   patient
   kind
   full of goodness
   trustful
   gentle
   self-controlled

   Expand on each of these in a way that is relevant to present-day situations.
2. Link up the list from St Paul with the list that people have already discovered in the first part of the session.
3. Explain that the Church is made up of fallible human beings! We attempt to live out these qualities in our

relationships with other people – we do not always succeed.

ABOUT OURSELVES

Give each person the list from St Paul on a piece of paper. Ask them to score themselves on these qualities. 'Give yourself one for excellent, two for good, three for fair, four for poor, five for hopeless! *Do not underestimate yourself!*' Ask people to share with each other their good or poor qualities as much as they wish.

How could we do better?

PRAYER TIME

Use 1 Corinthians 13:4–7 as a basis for a time of prayer.

1. Make sure that the correspondence between the list to be found in the writings of Paul and the list produced by the groups does coincide and is not forced in any way.
2. You might like to close the *Prayer time* with the Sign of Peace as an expression of our care for one another.

5. What does the Church say about sex?

AIM

The aim of this session is to help dispel misunderstanding regarding the Church's teaching on sex.

WHAT DO WE THINK THE CHURCH SAYS?:

Give each person the following list and ask them to fill it in. Stress that they will not have to show this to anyone.

The Church teaches that sex is a good thing.	True/Maybe/False
The Church teaches that the main reason for sex is to produce children.	True/Maybe/False
The Church teaches we shouldn't enjoy sex too much.	True/Maybe/False
The Church teaches that everyone	True/Maybe/False

(except priests and religious) are happier if they get married and that this is what God intends for people.

The Church teaches that sex out-   True/Maybe/False
side marriage is wrong.

The Church teaches it is not possi-   True/Maybe/False
ble to be a Catholic and to be 'on
the pill'.

The Church teaches that homo-   True/Maybe/False
sexuals are sinners because they
are homosexuals.

INPUT

1. Explain that very often the Church's teaching on sexual morality is misunderstood.
2. Take each of the statements and explain the Church's teaching about them. (There is some excellent material in easily digestible form in *How to Survive Being Married to a Catholic*, Redemptorist Publications, pp. 40–43.)

GROUP WORK

Linda and Wayne have been living together for three years. They set up home on a small private housing estate and purchased the house between them. They show no indication that they wish to get married now or in the future. They have recently joined the local parish church. What should be the attitude of the Christian community to them in the light of the Church's teaching that sex belongs within marriage? Should the community:

(a) ignore their present situation?
(b) challenge them with the Church's teaching by making it plain that if they wish to be full members of the community they must get married?
(c) refuse to have anything to do with them?
(d) adopt a different strategy altogether? (if so what?)

In small groups discuss what should be the Church's attitude to people such as Wayne and Linda.

PRAYER TIME

Thank God for all the gifts that he has given to us.
Thank him for the gift of the expression of love.

Sing: 'Now thank we all our God.'

Notes

1. This is not an easy session to handle. A great many misconceptions regarding the Church's teaching on sex are abroad.
2. Be sensitive to the position of those within the group. You may have people who are in situations such as Wayne and Linda. If so, you will need to adapt this.
3. Be sure that the impression given throughout the whole session is a positive one and does not reinforce a 'Thou Shalt Not' mentality.

6.　Justice – whose responsibility?

AIM

The aim of this session is to help people explore the theme of co-responsibility for justice in the wider world.

ABOUT OURSELVES

Have a large world map displayed for all to see. Encourage people to call out and mark on the map areas where they believe injustice is clearly visible.
    Explain the aim of the session.

GROUP WORK

Ask groups to outline what they think are gospel values.
    Allow time to gather this information together.

INPUT

(a)　If we look at the life of the people of Israel, justice was to be central to their community (e.g. Micah 6:8, Amos 5:24, etc.). It is to be central to the life of the Church, both universal and local, and to be the responsibility of all members.

(b)　The prophets rejected the idea that the cult (i.e. the worship of God) could be separated from justice towards other people. Our worship calls us to be just towards others.

(c) The call to be just extended beyond the confines of the community of Israel. Those outside the community were entitled to expect justice. We are responsible for standing up for those outside our communities who suffer injustice.

(d) Justice is linked with the dignity and rights of the individual and the community. Wherever dignity is abused or rights denied we must protest and do what we can to right the wrong.

(e) Living by gospel values means living out justice. We make up the Church, and so working for justice is the responsibility of every Christian.

(f) We need to find ways and means of working for justice in our own situations.

If time allows refer back to the world map.
   What can we do about injustice? (be practical)
   What areas of injustice do we see nearer to hand?
   What can we do?

PRAYER TIME

Gather around the map (have a lighted candle nearby).
   Give people a small votive candle.
   Encourage them to light the candle and to place it on or near an area of the world for which they wish to pray.
   Encourage people to pray for this situation at home.
   Say a prayer of commitment to work for justice.

Notes

1. There are plenty of references to justice scattered throughout the Scriptures (a good concordance will provide you with many examples).
2. Be prepared for questions about apparent injustice within the Church.
3. Be prepared to cope with the 'problem is too big for us to make any difference' approach. Stress the need for people to take responsibility however small it may be.
4. If it is possible, suggest that the group should choose one area they have discussed and prepare to take some collective action.

Chapter 7

TRAVELLING ON

Roy was convinced of the existence of God and had come to realize a long time ago that God was not a remote figure but part of his daily life. As an unemployed miner he knew what it was to struggle to make ends meet and the battle he had to stop himself falling into apathy or despair over his future – or lack of it.

Roy's faith had changed since redundancy. He had been forced to try and make sense of the changes in his own life and that of his family. He had to discover anew how God could be found in this new situation and how to live out his faith in a new way. He gained great strength from his friends at church. They admired the way he remained so cheerful and positive. Despite his lack of work Roy's faith gave him a sense of dignity. Even if he was unemployed he was still the same person and loved just as much.

Roy's belief in God also presented him with challenges in a world that, for him, had changed considerably since unemployment. As a Christian, how should he face the changes in his life and that of his family? How could he be free to believe in himself and his worthiness despite the fact that no one seemed to want his skills anymore? In what way could he share his faith with others in a similar position and with those in the Church? What good could he see in it all and how could he show it to others?

This chapter will look at the theme of 'Travelling On' in the faith. It contains material about the continuing journey in faith that we all make throughout our lives. It covers:

How does the journey of faith continue?
How can I grow in prayer?
How can I help others discover God's presence?
What responsibilities do I have?
How do I make choices?
What is my task?

1. How does the journey of faith continue?

AIM

The aim of this session is to help people explore the experience of new beginnings which are always involved in the journey of faith.

ABOUT OURSELVES

Either – one of the team members should tell the story of the change of direction which has happened to them,
Or – in pairs, invite people to discuss something from their own experience which involved a change in their lives.

Note

These need not be 'religious' events. It could be any new beginning in life, e.g. the birth of a baby, starting a new job or moving into a new area.

BRAINSTORM

List what sort of changes were made.

Also list what feelings and attitudes were involved in the change, e.g.

'I was afraid at first.'
'It was all so strange.'
'I was not sure I was good enough.'
'I was excited.'
'I didn't know what to expect.'

INPUT

Look at a number of biblical and other stories from the life of the Church to see the *type* of changes people made, *why* they made them and their *attitudes*.

Such stories might include:

Abraham   (Genesis 12:1–9)
Zacchaeus   (Luke 19:1–10)
The demoniac   (Mark 5:1–19)
Jonah   (The Book of Jonah)
St Francis
Mary   (Luke 1:26–38)

Draw out:

One change often leads to another – the journey goes on.

Changes enable us to grow in understanding.

Relationships involve us in give and take – it is the same with God. In our relationship with him he invites us to go on learning and so to go on changing.

There is a sense in which the end of one stage is the beginning of another.

GROUP WORK

Ask people to discuss:

Why do we find change so difficult?

What helps us to cope with new beginnings?

What help could the Church give us?

PRAYER TIME

Place a large candle in the middle of the group and invite people to spend a few moments reflecting on how the light of God has led them on their journey so far.

Close with a suitable hymn, e.g. 'Thy hand, O God, has guided', or a prayer thanking God for his guidance in the past and asking for his light to direct us in the future.

Notes

1. Notice the use of team members to tell their own stories in the first part of the session. This should be encouraged, as it helps people see a variety of ways in which God creates new beginnings for us.
2. Note that the new beginnings need not necessarily be religious. God is at work in all aspects of our lives.
3. Allow time for people to make comments at the end of the group work if necessary.

2. How can I grow in prayer?

AIM

The aim of this session is to enable people to experience two or three different ways of prayer.

INTRODUCTION

Explain to people that in this session we shall be experiencing three different ways of praying. Talk about:

(a) The necessity of variety in prayer. We do get stale some-times and need to find new ways of re-vitalizing ourselves in order that we may be open to God.

(b) Prayer is not something static. We go forwards (and sometimes feel as if we are going backwards) in our life of prayer. Compare it to a map on which there are hills and dales, rivers to cross, views to be enjoyed, etc.

(c) Prayer is challenging and demanding. It is not all about comfort and joy. The closer we come to God the more we see our own weaknesses and the more he challenges us to follow him.

(d) Explain carefully that it is unlikely people will find all three methods used during the evening helpful for them. Various temperaments prefer various methods of prayer. There is nothing wrong in this. We must find our own way and not copy other people's. Leave behind what is not suitable.

(e) Explain that these forms of prayer are for individual use. We are not dealing in this session with corporate or public prayer. Explain, too, that silence is an important part of these exercises. We need to allow God to speak to us as well as speaking to him.

1. USING THE IMAGINATION

Explain that this way of praying helps us to use that under-estimated gift, our imagination. As in all our methods we need time to bring ourselves consciously into the presence of God. Help people to sit comfortably and to spend time relaxing. Play some quiet music if this will help. Tell them consciously to bring any worries or problems they have before God and tell him about them and to ask silently for his guidance and an awareness of his presence.

Step 1
The leader gives everyone the following passage and then reads it slowly and prayerfully aloud.

He came out and went, as was his custom, to the Mount of Olives; and the disciples followed him. When he reached the place, he said to them, 'Pray that you may not come into the time of trial.' Then he withdrew from them about a stone's throw, knelt down, and prayed, 'Father, if you are willing, remove this cup from me; yet, not my will but yours be done.' When he got up from prayer, he came to the disciples and found them sleeping . . .

(Luke 22:39–42, 45)

Step 2

Ask people to read the text again to themselves, trying to picture the scene. When they have done this they should put the text away and imagine themselves there, as one of the disciples.

Allow some time for this and then help people to imagine the garden – what is it like – where is Jesus? etc.

Imagine the disciples – what do they feel – what do you feel as one of them? etc.

Imagine Jesus – how do you see him – what is he doing? etc.

These questions should be asked slowly and with periods of silence in between. Allow people time then to stay with the picture as long as it feels comfortable.

Step 3

The leader should now encourage people to form a short silent prayer.

Step 4

The leader will now pray for others, especially any known to the group who are distressed or in despair. This can be done aloud. The whole exercise should take no more than five minutes. When this is finished allow people time to express how they found it – what they enjoyed, what they disliked, how helpful it was or how unhelpful. What did they discover?

Have a cup of coffee or some other activity at this point. When the group reassembles, move into the second form of prayer. This is quite short.

USING A SENTENCE

Step 1
Encourage people to settle down once again into an attitude of openness.

Step 2
The leader should repeat several times the following quotation:

> Jesus said 'You did not choose me but I chose you. And I appointed you to go and bear fruit, fruit that will last, so that the Father will give you whatever you ask him in my name.'
>
> (John 15:16)

Step 3
People should say the sentence two or three times aloud together so that they can remember it without difficulty.

Step 4
When you are happy with this, ask people to repeat the sentence several times themselves in silence, putting the emphasis on the word 'I' ('*I* chose you. And I appointed you to go and bear fruit.')

Encourage people to ask 'What does it mean that *God* has chosen us?'

Step 5
Encourage people to repeat the sentence again, this time putting the emphasis on the word 'chose'.

What does it mean that God has *chosen* us?

Step 6
Continue this process, taking your time and emphasizing the words 'you', 'appointed you', 'to go', 'bear fruit'.

Step 7
Allow a short time of silence for people to sum up their meditation with a prayer of their own.

The leader should again draw out from people how they felt about this exercise – what was helpful and what was not helpful.

USING OUR EYES

If there is time and people are not too tired, use a third method of prayer. This one uses visual help.

Have a crucifix and a candle where all can see them. You may wish to use an icon instead of a crucifix or give people a card with a picture on it – anything that will help them concentrate their thoughts and use the picture as a means of communicating with God.

Step 1

Allow people time to look at the picture and think about what they like in it – or dislike! They can focus on the candle if they do not like the visual image offered to them.

Step 2

Allow people time to 'enter into' the picture themselves and to allow the picture to 'enter into them'. Encourage them to let the picture speak to them and to formulate any thoughts into a prayer.

Step 3

Stress that people should not be worried if they go off at a tangent. The way to deal with distractions is to turn them into prayer, not to try and ignore them. So encourage people to allow themselves just to be led.

As before, allow people time to make a response to this method of prayer and to discuss what they found helpful or unhelpful. There is no closing prayer for this session.

Notes

1. It is important that people are aware that there is no 'right way' of praying. God leads each person in the way that is right for him or her.
2. It is important to make it clear to people that these are forms of individual prayer which others have found useful but they are not exclusive. The use of the Rosary, set prayers and spoken prayers from the heart are other methods.
3. It may be that people find it helpful to pray in a group, in which case encourage them to do so on a regular basis!

('Using the imagination' and 'Using a sentence' are adapted from
Christine Dodd, *Making Scripture Work*, Geoffrey Chapman, 1989.)

3. How can I help others discover God's presence?

AIM

The aim of this session is to help people explore their own role
in sharing faith with others.

INPUT

This should contain two main points:

(a) *The uniqueness of each person*
    A member of the team should give one or two illustrations
    from his or her own life about how faith has been shared
    with them. This need not be very intense. One or two
    simple illustrations will do as long as they are clear. It
    should be pointed out that we all need others to share
    faith with us over and over again. The speaker should
    also point out the qualities or attitudes of the person shar-
    ing faith which impressed them in the experience. This
    should lead naturally on to the second part of the *input*.

(b) *The gift of ourselves*
    Two or three members of the team should now have a
    dialogue about how the gifts we have, help us to share
    faith with others. Simple illustrations should be used.
    They should affirm each other's gifts in a natural and
    'matter-of-fact' way and show how each of these gifts is
    used to build up faith.

GROUP WORK

Give each person a large piece of paper and a felt-tip pen and
ask them to draw themselves in the centre of the paper (this
can be quite light-hearted!). They should then express on paper
how faith has been shared with them and what gifts they have
to share faith with others. Impress upon people that artistic
ability is not important. Allow time for sharing of these pictures.

CONCLUSION

Draw together a list of the gifts that exist within the group.

Discuss together ways of using these gifts in order to share faith with others (be practical).

PRAYER TIME

Seat everyone in a circle. The leader should have a fairly large candle. Explain that this will be passed from person to person to express our sharing of faith with each other. Ask people to hold the candle for a few seconds and make a prayer of their own from what they have learned during this session and then to pass it on. During this, quiet music may be played.

Close with the Our Father.

Notes

1. Note the use of drawing in this session. People may feel very hesitant about this. Lots of encouragement may be needed.
2. Do not make the dialogue in the *Input* session too intense. This is not designed for mutual admiration but for a simple expression of the gifts that each speaker has.

4. What responsibilities do I have?

AIM

The aim of this session is to use a gospel story in order to help people uncover some of the responsibilities which come from following Christ.

THE GOSPEL STORY

Give everyone a copy of the following text:

> They came to the other side of the sea, to the country of the Gerasenes. And when he had stepped out of the boat, immediately a man out of the tombs with an unclean spirit met him. He lived among the tombs; and no one could restrain him any more, even with a chain; for he had often been restrained with shackles and chains, but the chains he wrenched apart, and the shackles he broke in pieces; and no one had the strength to subdue him. Night and day among the tombs and on the mountains he was always howling and bruising himself with stones. When he saw Jesus from a distance, he ran and bowed down before him; and he shouted at the

top of his voice, 'What have you to do with me, Jesus, Son of the Most High God? I adjure you by God, do not torment me.' For he had said to him, 'Come out of the man, you unclean spirit!' Then Jesus asked him, 'What is your name?' He replied, 'My name is Legion; for we are many.' He begged him earnestly not to send them out of the country. Now there on the hillside a great herd of swine was feeding; and the unclean spirits begged him, 'Send us into the swine; let us enter them.' So he gave them permission. And the unclean spirits came out and entered the swine; and the herd, numbering about two thousand, rushed down the steep bank into the sea, and were drowned in the sea.

The swineherds ran off and told it in the city and in the country. Then people came to see what it was that had happened. They came to Jesus and saw the demoniac sitting there, clothed and in his right mind, the very man who had had the legion; and they were afraid. Those who had seen what had happened to the demoniac and to the swine reported it. Then they began to beg Jesus to leave their neighbourhood. As he was getting into the boat, the man who had been possessed by demons begged him that he might be with him. But Jesus refused, and said to him, 'Go home to your friends, and tell them how much the Lord has done for you, and what mercy he has shown you.'

(Mark 5:1–19)

Arrange the seating in the form of a square with one end left open (i.e. three sides of a square). Divide the people into three groups and ask them to sit in these three areas. People should be facing inwards towards the centre of the square. Ask one group to imagine themselves as the demoniac. Ask a second group to imagine themselves as the people of the surrounding area and the third group to think of themselves as Jesus. Allow people time to read carefully through the story and to immerse themselves in the character they are to think about. The leader should then go through the story verse by verse drawing out from people how they felt as the story progresses. This can be done quite simply by asking questions (e.g. ask the people playing the townsfolk how they felt when Jesus arrived among them – how did Jesus feel to be there?). The groups are not allowed to interact with each other. All must be channelled through the leader. As the story progresses, draw out the attitude of Jesus towards the man and the attitude of the townspeople towards him. This should flow quite naturally from the experience of going through the story. Encourage people to act in character (i.e. 'I did this when Jesus arrived' rather than 'I think the demoniac did this when Jesus arrived').

When you have reached the end of the passage allow people to discuss what new things they gained out of the experience. Make sure they are 'de-roled' before progressing to the next section.

INPUT

The leader of this section should concentrate on what the passage has told us about Jesus' attitude to this man. It should include:

(a) Jesus *accepts* this person even though others have rejected him.
(b) Jesus *respects* this man's dignity. He is tolerant both to him and to the townspeople.
(c) Jesus *sees the injustice* of the situation and wishes to right it.
(d) Jesus shows *compassion* to the man.
(e) Jesus *gives him* a task to do.

The leader should link up each of these attitudes of Jesus to our own experience of trying to be his followers and to act like him. Emphasis should be placed on our responsibility to act with these characteristics.

GROUP WORK

How can we put what we have learned during this session into practice?

PRAYER TIME

Have a large poster or picture of a 'disadvantaged person or group'. (Suitable posters can be obtained from CAFOD, Christian Aid, etc.) Allow people a time to reflect on their responsibilities towards this person or group.

Conclude with a prayer of forgiveness for all we have not done to enhance their dignity and for the grace to serve them better in the future. (Make sure this prayer is not patronizing towards the less-fortunate members of our society.)

Notes

1. When using the Bible passage try not to get too tied down with questions about demons and pigs! Explain the beliefs of the time but concentrate on the attitude of Jesus to this man and his power to release him from whatever held him captive. You may wish to talk about all of us being enslaved to some form of captivity.
2. Allow people to draw out what they see in the passage for themselves. Keep in mind the aim of the session and do not 'force' the comments you want out of people.
3. Allow time for some feedback from the groups if you feel this is necessary.

5. How do I make choices?

AIM

The aim of this session is to enable people to see that making choices in the light of the gospel is an on-going process.

ABOUT OURSELVES

Provide a range of newspapers and magazines and ask people to discover stories where the making of choices is involved. This might be done in small groups. What elements affected the choices made? When people have had a chance to discover stories and to think about the question, list their responses so that all can see.

INPUT

Share with the group some of the questions we need to ask ourselves when making choices.

(a) Is what we intend to do *true to the gospel?* Would Jesus approve? Is what we intend to do 'good news'?
(b) Is the choice we intend to make *in accordance with the experience of Christians who have gone before us*? Are we intending to do or say something which is against Church teaching? Does what we intend to do or say have a unifying or a divisive effect on the church community of which we are part?
(c) Is the choice in accordance with our *conscience?* Is our 'inner voice' telling us this is right or wrong?

(d)   What are the *social and cultural issues* involved in the choices we make?

We need to consider all four areas when we make a decision.

GROUP WORK

Divide into smaller groups and give each group one of the three following case studies. Ask the group to apply the criteria above to each of the cases. What choice would they make and why?

Case study one

Anne's daughter Mandy has been 'going steady' with her boyfriend for three months. She lives at home and Sam lives the other side of town. Sam works for a small engineering firm which is feeling the effects of a small order book. He is not sure how long he will be able to keep his job. One day Mandy arrives home and announces to Anne that she and Sam have obtained a flat and intend to live together. She says she does not know if she will eventually marry Sam. Mandy knows her mother probably will not approve of this arrangement but she intends to go ahead even though her relationship with Sam is sometimes stormy. Anne does not wish to break communication with her daughter but she does want to make her feelings about the situation felt. On the one hand she does not approve of Mandy and Sam's action and feels she must say so, on the other hand, she does not want to alienate either of them. What should she do?

Case study two

Richard is in a dilemma. He has a job, which basically he does not enjoy but which pays well. He has the chance to move to a position where he will be much happier but where the salary is very much lower. If Richard had been single or could manage on the lower pay without causing harm to his family his decision would be easier, but the choice is between less money for the family with the consequent tightening of the belt and the fact that a new job would make him much less irritable and touchy for them to live with. He has to weigh up the financial considerations and the fact that his family may have to choose between more money with a miserable Richard, or less money and a happier Richard. If he goes for the latter, will his family cope with the tensions a tight budget will bring or will they end up as miserable as he is now? If he goes for the former can they cope with his irritability and tension? Which should he choose?

Case study three

When Gary was given the sack, Sarah was furious. She had worked with him for almost six years and felt his dismissal was unfair. 'It's just a cost-cutting operation', she said. The management claim that Gary was a consistently slow worker was not really true. It was the injustice of the situation that made Sarah so cross. 'He may be a bit slow but his work is adequate and he always stays until he gets the job done', said Sarah. 'They can hardly complain if the job is done in the end.' The other people in Sarah's office said she should not make a fuss or she could well find herself without a job. She was in a dilemma. Her family were not dependent on her for the money but it was a great help to them. Could she take the risk of facing the issue or should she just keep quiet? What should she do?

Allow people plenty of time to work with these case studies and draw together the results.

PRAYER TIME

Read the story of the rich young man – Matthew 19:16–22.

Ask people to reflect in silence on what they would have done if they had been the rich young man.

Close with a prayer asking for courage to follow the call of Christ and to make the right choices in our lives.

(Case Study 2 adapted from Christine Dodd, *The Immortal Diamond*, Darton, Longman and Todd.)

6. What is my task?

AIM

The aim of this session is to help people think about their unique role within the Church and the way they are to exercise it.

It is a good idea to have one session which introduces people in the group to those in the local church who hold various positions of responsibility or who have particular expertise in one part of the ministry of the church.

This can be done in the form of a social gathering, with various individuals having a few minutes each to speak to the group about their particular role or the work of their organization.

Allow plenty of space and time for people to chat informally and for contact to be established. Encourage people to become involved.

Notes

1. Ideally this session needs to follow one which deals with the importance of our talents and gifts and our responsibility to use them in the service of God.
2. Make sure people do not feel they *have* to join a particular group or be involved in a particular way. Other avenues are open to people.
3. Make sure people do not think that the only way of serving God is directly through the Church. Involvement in other groups and non-religious organizations is important. It would be a good idea to have another session which deals with this and where the work of various non-church organizations is explained.

SUGGESTED RESOURCES

General Books on RCIA

Rite of Christian Initiation of Adults (London: Geoffrey Chapman, 1987).

Peter Ball, *Journey into Faith* (London: SPCK, 1984).

Patricia Barbernitz, *RCIA, What It Is, How It Works* (Liguori Publications, 1983).

Becoming a Catholic Christian: A Symposium on Christian Initiation (New York: Sadlier, 1978).

Henri Bourgeois, *On Becoming Christian: Christian Initiation and Its Sacraments* (Athlone, Ireland: St Paul Publications, 1984).

Kenneth Boyack, CSP, *A Parish Guide to Adult Initiation* (Mahwah, NJ: Paulist Press, 1980).

Creating a Living and Missionary Parish: A Brief Guide to the Rite of Christian Initiation of Adults (London: Office of Evangelization).

Michael Dujarier, *The Rites of Christian Initiation: Historical and Pastoral Reflections* (New York: Sadlier, 1979).

James B. Dunning, *New Wine, New Wineskins: Implications of the RCIA for Parish Life* (New York: Sadlier, 1981).

'Evangelization in the Modern World' (English translation of Pope Paul VI, Apostolic Exhortation *Evangelii Nuntiandi*) (London: Catholic Truth Society, 1976).

Aidan Kavanagh, *The Shape of Baptism: The Rite of Christian Initiation* (Pueblo, 1978).

Raymond B. Kemp, *A Journey in Faith: An Experience of the Catechumenate* (New York: Sadlier, 1979).

Ron Lewinski, *Guide for Sponsors* (revised ed.) (Chicago: Liturgy Training Publications, 1983).

Ron Lewinski, *Welcoming the New Catholic* (revised ed.) (Chicago: Liturgy Training Publications, 1981).

Brian McEvoy, *On Becoming a Catholic Christian – Introduction to the RCIA* (London: The Catholic Enquiry Centre).

On Becoming a Catholic Christian: An Introduction to the Rite of Christian Initiation of Adults (London: Office of Evangelization).

Mark Searle, *Christening: The Making of Christians* (Bury St Edmunds: Kevin Mayhew, 1980).

History

Michael Dujarier, *A History of the Catechumenate – The First Six Centuries* (New York: Sadlier, 1979).

Anne Field OSB, *New Life – What It Meant to Become a Christian in the Early Church* (London: Mowbray, 1977)

Edward Yarnold SJ, *The Awe-inspiring Rites of Initiation* (Athlone, Ireland: St Paul, 1971).

Resources for the catechetical content of RCIA

A New Catechism (The Dutch Catechism) (London: Burns & Oates).

W. Bausch, *A New Look at the Sacraments* (Mystic, CT: XXIII Publications).

Nigel Bavidge, *The Sacraments Explained* (Bury St Edmunds: Kevin Mayhew).

William Brown, *R.C.I.A. – A Practical Approach to Christian Initiation of Adults.*

Michael Fewell, *The Way We Were* (London: T. Shand).

Tad Guzie, *Jesus and the Eucharist* (Mystic, CT: XXIII Publications).

Tad Guzie, *The Book of Sacramental Basics* (Bury St Edmunds: Kevin Mayhew).

John Hardon SJ, *The Catholic Catechism* (London: Geoffrey Chapman).

Deborah M. Jones, *Focus on Faith* (Bury St Edmunds: Kevin Mayhew).

Hugh Lavery, *Reflections on the Creed* (Athlone, Ireland: St Paul).

R. Lawler OFM Cap *et al.* (eds), *The Teaching of Christ – A Catholic Catechism for Adults* (Dublin: Veritas).

Gerald O'Mahoney SJ, *Abba, Father – A Personal Catechism of the Catholic Faith* (Athlone, Ireland: St Paul).

Marvyn Tower, *Deepening the Roots – A Parish Adult Education Programme Based on RCIA* (Birmingham: Maryvale Catechetical Centre).

Anthony Wilhelm, *Christ Among Us – A Modern Presentation of the Catholic Faith* (Mahwah, NJ: Paulist Press).

Resources for the participant

Believing in Jesus – A Popular Overview of the Catholic Faith (St Anthony Press).

Richard Chilson, *An Introduction to the Faith of Catholics* (Mahwah, NJ: Paulist Press).

Paul Guerin, *I Believe.*

Handbook for Today's Catholic Beliefs, Practices and Prayers (A Redemptorist Pastoral Publication).

How to Survive Being Married to a Catholic (A Redemptorist Publication, 1985).

John Retford, *What Catholics Believe* (London: CTS).

The Illustrated Catechism – Catholic Beliefs in Words and Pictures (A Redemptorist Pastoral Publication).

Your Faith – A Practical Presentation of Catholic Belief and Sacramental Life (A Redemptorist Pastoral Publication).